MOUNT
TEL. 051

KU-562-748

MARKETING
AND
COMPETITIVE SUCCESS

Michael J. Baker and Susan J. Hart

WITHDRAWN

Philip Allan

New York London Toronto Sydney Tokyo

LIVERPOOL POLYTECHNIC LIBRARY

3 1111 00300 3348

First published 1989 by
Philip Allan
66 Wood Lane End, Hemel Hempstead,
Hertfordshire, HP2 4RG
A division of
Simon & Schuster International Group

© Michael J. Baker and Susan J. Hart, 1989

All rights reserved. No part of this publication may be
reproduced, stored in a retrieval system, or transmitted, in any
form, or by any means, electronic, mechanical, photocopying,
recording or otherwise, without the prior permission, in
writing, from the publisher.

Printed and bound in Great Britain by
Billing & Sons Ltd, Worcester

Library of Congress Cataloging-in-Publication Data

Baker, Michael John.
   Marketing and competitive success/Michael Baker and Susan Hart.
     p. cm.
   ISBN 0-86003-566-2.   ISBN 0-86003-665-0 (pbk.)
   1. Marketing. 2. Success in business. I. Hart, Susan.
   II. Title.
HF5415.B277 1989
   658.8-dc 19   88-38568
                                                 CIP

British Library Cataloguing-in-Publication Data

Baker, Michael J.
   Marketing and competitive success
   1. Business firms. Marketing
   I. Title   II. Hart, Susan
   658.8

ISBN 0-86003-566-2
ISBN 0-86003-665-0 Pbk

1 2 3 4 5   93 92 91 90 89

Contents

Preface

Without a doubt the issue of competitiveness has dominated the managerial thinking and practice of the 1980s and there is no reason to believe that this preoccupation will lessen as we move into the 1990s. In this book we seek to document the developments — social, economic and technological — which have given rise to this concern, together with managerial responses to the challenges such changes present. More specifically, we are concerned with establishing the role which marketing has to play in contributing to the competitive success of firms, industries and, ultimately, nations.

In Chapter 1 we seek to define the nature of marketing as both a managerial orientation towards the management of the whole enterprise and as a business function, as a preliminary to exploring its contribution to competitive performance. The nature of competitiveness is then defined as a basis for examining the comparative performance of British manufacturing industry in the post-World War II period. The analysis makes dismal reading and underlines the need for radical action if the UK is to regain its status as a major trading nation.

Chapter 2 provides a review of the main theories of international trade from mercantilism to modern technology gap and life cycle explanations of international competition. This survey is reinforced by a short reprise of theories of competition from which it is concluded that, with ever increasing productivity as a consequence of task specialisation and technological innovation, and a slowing of population growth, the supply capacity of the advanced economies is now equal to or even exceeds the available demand.

Faced with such a situation, individual firms and industries must find ways of differentiating their output so that consumers can develop a preference for it over other competing products and services. In the process the emphasis moves from standardisation to differentiation, from homogeneity to heterogeneity, from price to non-price factors and from production to marketing.

These themes are picked up in Chapter 3, which draws heavily upon an article which first appeared in the *Welsh Business Review*; this details the most significant changes that have occurred in the past forty years. Dominant among these changes are the emergence of consumerism in the 1950s and 1960s with its overtones of anti-business attitudes, the emergence of Japan and West Germany as world class economic powers, and the rise of the Newly Industrialising Countries. Together with the energy crises of the 1970s these events resulted in the unsettled and disordered period of turbulence which resulted in a major shake-out in many industries in many countries. In turn, this gave rise to the focus on the nature and sources of competitive success.

Chapter 4 comprises an extensive and wide-ranging review of the voluminous literature concerned with factors considered critical to success, with a particular emphasis upon the role and contribution of marketing. Our review indicates that, while many authors endorse the importance of a marketing orientation, few do so in any specific way which could be implemented operationally. A second conclusion is that many of the works purporting to explain the secrets of competitive success are severely flawed in that they are specific to individual firms or industries at a given point in time, depend heavily on anecdotal and subjective evidence, and fail to determine whether the properties associated with successful firms are absent from unsuccessful firms. Without the latter information it is difficult to know what advice to offer the unsuccessful firm!

Chapters 5 and 6 describe original empirical research undertaken at Strathclyde University designed to address some of the major deficiencies identified in earlier work on the subject. In the event, our data show that there are comparatively few factors which are present in successful firms and absent from less successful ones. In part we conclude this is so because all in our sample are 'survivors' of the shake-out but, perhaps more important, the main conclusion to be drawn seems to be that 'It's not what you do, it's the way that you do it'.

In Chapters 7 and 8 we seek to determine what defines quality, particularly in terms of the implementation of corporate strategy. Chapter 7 suggests that we are in a process of transition from an industrial society, with an emphasis upon mass consumption and materialism, to a knowledge-based society in which quality will take precedence over quantity. In order to respond to the challenge this presents, Chapter 8 proposes that we need to accomplish a major attitude or culture change and that, in a competitive context, this calls for recognition of consumer sovereignty and the development of and commitment to a marketing orientation.

The authors would like to thank the organisations which funded the research: the Chartered Institute of Marketing, the Design Council (Scotland), the Economic and Social Research Council and the Scottish Development Agency; the editors and publishers of the journals and books in which some of the ideas presented here have been presented previously; our secretaries, and particularly Mrs June Peffer and Mrs Joan McGovern, for transcribing our often illegible jottings; our colleagues, Ms Jean Kidd and Christine Reid at the Business Information Centre, for helping us find our way through the maze of published statistics and business reports; and last, but not least, all the managers who participated in our surveys and made the project possible.

M.J. Baker   *University of Strathclyde*
S.J. Hart   *May 1989*

1
Marketing and Competitiveness

1.1 Introduction

On Friday, 25 November 1988 the British Government reported the biggest ever deficit on a single month's international trade (£2.4 billion) and Bank Rates rose a further 1 per cent to 13 per cent. Cause for real concern or temporary imbalance? — only time will tell. But for managers who have lived through the turbulence of the 1970s, survived the shakeout of the early eighties and been carried along on the tide of prosperity which succeeded this, the doubts must remain. After a period of years of low inflation and high economic growth are we once again to experience a return to the short-term, stop—go policies of the previous decade, or has our recent success been built upon sounder foundations?

Given the range and quality of advice available to governments, and recognising the differences of opinion which exist among such advisers, it is unlikely that any single analysis will provide an answer to such a complex and difficult question. Our purpose is more modest: it seeks to address the more focused issue of the role which marketing has to play in improving competitiveness.

In his guest editorial to the Winter (1988) edition of the *Journal of Marketing Management*, devoted to the theme of competitiveness, Professor John Saunders (1988) of Loughborough University observed that

> In 1981 the National Economic Development Office concluded that 'Lack of expertise in marketing is the single most important cause of the disappointing performance of British companies in the last two decades.' Despite Britain's much improved economic performance in the mid 1980s there is still cause for concern. Paradoxically, the

1

record gains achieved in cost reduction, productivity and real profits have not been complemented by improved market performance. *Britain is the only industrial nation to have experienced an absolute decline in manufacturing sales since 1977* [author's emphasis].

In the same issue, Arthur Francis and Diana Winstanley (1988) had the following to say:

> The increased competitive pressure (or perhaps, more accurately, an increase in managers' awareness of that pressure) can be traced back to the 1979–81 period when the combination of the high pound sterling, high interest rates, and recession induced by the second oil price rise reduced the competitiveness of UK manufacturing industry to the point where nearly 20% of its capacity was knocked out. For many of those firms which survived, this trauma led to their investigating new ways of developing and maintaining a competitive edge. Organisational re-structuring and new management techniques were two elements of many firms' recovery strategy.

Given the emphasis upon *marketing* as a source of competitive success and the stress placed upon the need for firms to adopt the marketing concept and become *marketing orientated*, one is entitled to inquire why our competitive performance has not improved. Is marketing a panacea for all competitive ills, or is it just a placebo, belief in which may provide temporary relief to one's symptoms but do nothing to address the underlying causes of one's declining competitive health? In this book we seek to provide at least some answers to this question. In doing so it is not our intention to offer an extended philosophical explanation of the nature of marketing but, rather, to examine how and why changes in competition have resulted in a switch in emphasis from supply to demand and from producer to consumer. That said, it will be helpful, in this introductory chapter, to provide some definitions of marketing and competitiveness as a background to our analysis of the contribution of marketing to competitive success.

1.2 What is Marketing?

In the *Macmillan Dictionary of Marketing and Advertising* (1984) we observed that there is no single, universally agreed definition of marketing but a whole spectrum which reflects the diversity of perspectives adopted by different authors. On closer examination, however, it becomes clear that the common thread which links all the definitions together is an emphasis upon 'mutually satisfying exchange relationships'. This being so, it is ironic that we think of marketing as being a relatively recent innovation when clearly it is, or was, the basis of the very first barter exchanges, when individuals discovered that they could improve their quality of life by exchanging surpluses arising from their own specialised activities for surpluses arising from other people's different specialisations. Thus the history of economic growth and development is founded upon the concepts of task specialisation and exchange, facilitated by the application of technology and management.

Until comparatively recently, however, natural population growth, and the almost insatiable appetite of consumers for more and better products, has meant that demand has exceeded supply. It was not until the 1950s that accelerating technology and a slowing of population growth resulted in the world's most affluent economy facing up to the problem that it could create excess supplies of most goods and services. This represented a waste of the scarce natural resources which economies are meant to use to maximise the satisfaction of their members, and it called for a radical reappraisal of the relationship between supply and demand. This reappraisal was precipitated not only by unsold inventories in producers' factories and warehouses, but also by a swelling volume of criticism generally labelled as *consumerism*.

Consumerism manifested itself in many forms, from the sophisticated criticisms of materialism in John Kenneth Galbraith's *The Affluent Society* to the populist writings of Vance Packard in books like *The Waste Makers* and *The Hidden Persuaders*.

Many have claimed that consumerism is the shame of marketing — our own view is the opposite. Consumerism is a cry for help and the rediscovery of the concept of mutually satisfying exchange relationships in which both parties receive the benefits and satisfactions they are seeking. When producer and consumer bargain face to face in the market-place they have only themselves to blame (assuming the absence of fraud) if they enter into an unsatisfactory bargain. But in the pursuit of economies of production and distribution to satisfy the rapidly growing demand of expanding populations, production becomes concentrated and producers are physically separated from consumers. As long as demands are basic and simple, and exceed — or are equal to — the supply capacity, then output will be absorbed and give at least the semblance that producers are satisfying consumers. But what happens when the supply capacity exceeds effective demand? — increased competition, reduced margins and profitability and, for some producers, failure.

However, while some producers will decline and fail, others will grow and prosper. The latter are seen as being more 'competitive' than the former and it is the nature of this competitive edge which has resulted in the rediscovery of marketing as a philosophy of business, which stresses the need to base production decisions upon carefully defined consumer needs. Thus, as Peter Drucker pointed out in *The Practice of Management* (1954), 'Marketing is not only much broader than selling, it is not a specialised activity at all. It encompasses the entire business. It is the whole business seen from the point of view of its final result, that is, from the customer's point of view.'

It was this theme which Ted Levitt picked up in his seminal 'Marketing Myopia' and has reinforced more recently in *The Marketing Imagination* in which he states: 'The purpose of a business is not to make profits but to create and keep customers. Customers are a company's most valuable asset, and only a marketing orientated corporate strategy can build and manage that asset well.' And later: 'People buy solutions to problems, not products, and successful marketers are problem solvers. They differentiate their products/services from the competition with tangible features and intangible promises and metaphors that present customers with the answers to their problems.' In other words, marketing assumes a dialogue between producer and consumer, from which both parties expect to derive satisfaction which is meaningful to them in terms of their own objectives. In the chapters which follow it will emerge that while the concept is simple, if not self-evident, it is its implementation which will largely lead to success or failure. However, before developing this proposition in greater detail it will be helpful to define competitiveness and review some of the evidence which supports the view that UK Ltd. has suffered a long-term structural decline in terms of its ability to compete in world markets for manufactured goods.

1.3 What is Competitiveness?

Before looking at the recent competitive history of UK manufacturing, it is useful to state precisely what we take competitiveness to mean, since it can be used to cover a number of related concepts. Confusion arises because the definition of competitiveness is often expressed in terms of two related, but different, concepts: *how to measure competitiveness* and/or *what affects competitiveness*.

The meaning of competitiveness is further obscured by the reluctance of many commentators to state the actual *'level'* to which they refer, for competitiveness can clearly be aggregated to a number of levels: the national level, the industry level, the company level and the product level. Hence we are all used to reading about competitive countries, industries, companies and products. Taking competitiveness as it applies to two of these levels (national and company levels) together with how commentators approach its definition, (measurement of competitiveness and factors affecting competitiveness) the complexity of the concept becomes all too apparent (see Table 1.1).

The division between the levels, however, is somewhat artificial in that competitiveness is an advantage which may be derived

Table 1.1 How Competitiveness is Defined

	Factors affecting competitiveness	*How to measure competitiveness*
Company	Ownership Asset base Marketing skill Marketing resource R & D expenditure New product development (NPD) Cost base Managerial quality	Profit ratios Sales measures Market share Export growth
Nation	Training Education R & D support Cost base Productivity	Share of world trade Balance of trade Export growth Manufacturing's share of total output

from price, quality, speed of delivery, or design which enables a company or a nation to secure sales at the expense of its rivals.

Implicit in this notion is the contention that the competitiveness of a nation (or a company) depends on how well the factors relating to its products or services satisfy the demand criteria of particular markets in comparison to the offerings of other companies or nations. Also, as can be seen from Table 1.1, some of the factors said to influence competitiveness are common to both levels: cost base being an example.

In any case, a nation's competitiveness is itself dependent upon the competitiveness of those companies that operate within its borders — a simple truth often omitted by academic writers. Indeed the ability to defend one's own home market against foreign competition is one of the best measures of that country's ability to succeed in other markets. Equally, the division between the factors affecting competitiveness and those used to measure it is not entirely distinct. Frequently, factors which *affect* competitiveness are often used as *surrogate measures* of competitiveness. For example, Scibberas (1986) uses the amount of patenting not as something likely to affect competitiveness (through the likely introduction of new products), but as evidence *of* competitiveness.

In measuring company competitiveness a number of concepts are commonly used. The simplest measure is the achievement of the company's objectives, which can vary from financial measures to targets related to innovation and technology. However, the most common type of company objectives are financial — for example, sales volume, market share and return on investment. Indeed, publications like *Times 1000* and *Fortune 500*, which rank companies in terms of their performance, all use financial measures such as sales turnover, pre-tax profit, share prices and return on shareholders' funds.

Many of the studies that have been designed to test what it is that distinguishes competitive companies have used financial criteria as measures of competitive performance. One of the best known examples is that of Peters and Waterman (1982). They used seven criteria to define excellent company performance. Three are measures of growth and long-term wealth creation over a twenty-year period and three are measures of return on capital and sales. The seventh criterion is based on the company's history of innovativeness. Goldsmith and Clutterbuck (1984) define competitive companies using three measures: (i) high growth in assets, turnover and profits over the past ten years; (ii) a consistent reputation within the industrial sector as a leader, and (iii) a good, solid public reputation. Hooley, Lynch and West (1984) isolate the top 10 per cent of their sample of companies, based on measures of pre-tax profits, ROI and market share, and call them high-fliers. Chapter 5 reviews these measures more fully.

At the national level, the most common *measures* of competitiveness are those that relate to *trading performance*, of which there are four major examples. The first is a country's share in world trade. This can of course be broken down by industry sector to compare performance of traditional (read declining) industries and new (read growth) industries. A second familiar measure is made up of import penetration and the amount of goods a country exports: the balance of trade. In the case of Britain, this has caused concern for many years and continues to do so.

There are a number of criticisms of these two measures. With respect to a nation's share of world trade, it has been argued that any decline may not be due to a decline in export performance, but rather because of more and more countries participating in world trade, thereby reducing any one nation's share of it (Harrod 1967, Francis 1986, 1987, Krugman and Hatsopoulos 1987 and Buckley *et al.* 1988). Likewise, increasing import penetration experienced by a country need not necessarily mean decline if it reflects its increasing participation in world trade. In any case, it could be argued that both these measures are subject to government policy regarding interest and exchange rates and therefore are not *only* the direct result of the competitiveness of a nation's business community.

The third measure is that of export growth which attempts to measure the real increase, if any, in a nation's exports. As this is a largely non-comparative way of looking at a nation's exports, it avoids the criticisms levelled at both the trade balance and share of world exports as reasonable indicators of a country's competitiveness (Thirwall 1982). This said, assessing anything in a vacuum is less than satisfactory.

The fourth measure of national competitiveness is manufacturing industry's share of total output; this measure is the subject

MOUNT PLEASANT LIBRARY
TEL. 051 207 3581 Ext. 3701

of much controversy. On the one hand are those who condemn the relative decline in a nation's manufacturing sector (Prowse 1985, and Krugman and Hatsopoulos 1987). Their main arguments include:

- As they are less tradeable than manufactures, services cannot hope to pay for imported goods.
- Services ride on the back of manufacturing, and yet they cannot exist without the latter.

Counter to these views are the following:

- Trade in services is increasing, therefore manufacturing's *share* of output is *bound* to decrease.
- Services *are* tradeable; the extent to which this is so is likely to grow.
- Service industries can buy in the goods they require in their operations.

No doubt the debate on these four measures of national competitiveness will smoulder on — each with its peculiar advantages and drawbacks. However, when any nation falls foul of *all four* (as is the case in Britain), it is necessary to look at its industrial performance in greater detail. While academics and politicians argue about their appropriateness or otherwise, the human and social costs of declining exports and share of world trade, increasing imports, and a devastated manufacturing industry have been enormous. The extent of the decline in the UK's economic performance is the subject of the next section.

1.4 The Competitiveness of British Manufacturing Industry

If we pick any one of the measures of competitiveness described above, then the UK economy does not appear to have been very healthy for the past quarter of a century. The evidence in support of this claim is overwhelming — it also makes for dry, dull and often depressing reading. Accordingly, we have selected only a few indicators to make our point and have collated the figures and tables in appendices to the chapter for those who wish to refer to them.

First, taking the UK share of world exports of manufactures, we see a steady and, at times, precipitous decline. From a share of 27.5 per cent in 1911–13, it fell to 18.5 per cent in the period 1931–38, where it remained (roughly) until the late 1950s (Pollard 1980). By 1965, the figure had fallen further to 13.9 per cent and 5 years later was trailing at less than 10 per cent (Karel *et al.* 1983). The pattern since 1976 is depicted in Appendix 1 — the decline continues.

Although Britain's share of world exports has decreased throughout the twentieth century, her total exports *in absolute terms* has remained steady (Francis 1986). Consultation of government figures detailing absolute export output show that, until 1964, growth in export volume was substantial and in excess of import volume (NEDO 1965). Since then, however, the tendency has been for export growth to slow down considerably (CSO 1988): exports as a percentage of sales actually decreased, between 1975 and 1985, in four out of the ten industry categories shown in Appendix 2, and remained almost static in chemicals and food and beverages. If we compare these figures with those of West Germany, France and Italy (see Appendix 3), in none of the industry categories do the British figures compare favourably.

While an absolute measure shows that British companies have, on the whole, kept their export sales up, the same is not true of their domestic sales. In the 1950s UK manufacturers virtually dominated their home market, with import penetration staying under 7 per cent into the 1960s. Over the period from 1968 to 1980, the ratio of imports of manufactures increased from 15 to 25 per cent (Karel *et al.* 1983). As shown by the analysis carried out in *Barclays Review* in 1983, which is reproduced in Appendix 4, import penetration increased dramatically between the years of 1970 and 1980, producing a deficit for the first time ever in 1983. It appears that while manufacturers are maintaining — and increasing — their export sales in certain industry sectors, the trend in import penetration seems, if anything, to be increasing. The Central Statistical Office's publication *Economic Trends* (1988) gives details of the continued increase in goods imported to the UK, as summarised by Appendix 5 (CSO 1988). This is further explored in Appendices 6 and 7, both of which show the extent to which this trend has been diffused throughout many sectors of British manufacturing industry. Even more interesting is the fact that the countries of origin of these imports are not confined to the newly industrialising world and its reputation as low-cost producer, as shown by Appendix 8.

Finally, the size of the manufacturing sector in British industry is smaller than for all its major competitors. While this is due, in part, to a healthy and expanding services sector, there has also been an absolute decline in manufacturing which has been 60 per cent steeper in the UK than in the rest of the developed world (Harvey-Jones 1986).

1.5 Conclusion

While some time has been spent in the preceding pages acknowledging the pitfalls of some of the measures of performance, the examples of industries are not merely the result of esoteric national book-keeping. These industries, along with many others, once provided healthy figures for the trade balance and many communities depended on them. However measured, the decline of British manufacturing has had real and tragic effects and the trend must be reversed.

While the main national and company measures of competitiveness have been outlined to expose the nature of the problem, the remainder of this book deals with those factors that influence company competitiveness, and it explores what management can do to secure the survival and growth of those companies for which it is responsible. Although such factors relate to a diversity of disciplines, our primary focus will be the contribution of marketing to competitive success.

Specifically, Chapter 2 reviews the various sources of competitiveness in some detail. It explores the nature of comparative advantage and its emphasis on relative costs and prices of homogeneous products. In contrast to this view is set the impact of increasing technological innovation: its ability to enhance supply capability and the potential to compete through non-price factors. Chapter 3 analyses how supply—demand equilibriums have been reflected in changing managerial orientations: production, sales and now marketing. Chapter 4 focuses on current thinking and practice regarding those factors which managers can manipulate to enhance the competitive success of their companies. Particular attention is given to studies which have investigated the managerial practices leading to success.

Chapter 5 describes two surveys, undertaken at Strathclyde University, that are designed to overcome some of the problems inherent in the studies examined in Chapter 4. Chapter 6 reports the surveys' findings and assesses the difficulties in identifying factors which truly differentiate between success and failure.

Chapter 7 synthesises the factors underlying competitive success. Given increased affluence, accelerating technology and rising expectations, customer satisfaction will depend upon a more focused and flexible marketing strategy. Chapter 8 concludes that a sustainable competitive advantage depends not only on what is done in a company, but also on the quality of execution.

Appendix: Economic Indicators

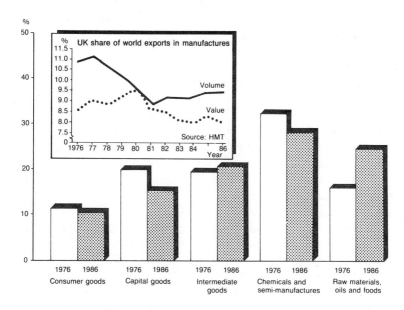

Source: NEDC (1987) *British Industrial Performance and International Competitiveness Over Recent Years.*

Appendix 1 UK Share of World Exports in Manufactures

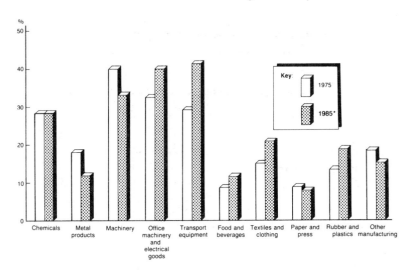

Source: NEDC (1987) *British Industrial Performance.*

Note: * or latest available year.

Appendix 2 Exports as a Percentage of Sales (UK)

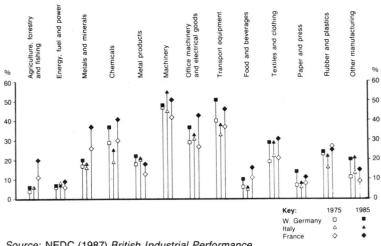

Source: NEDC (1987) *British Industrial Performance.*

Appendix 3 Exports as a Percentage of Sales in W. Germany, Italy
and France

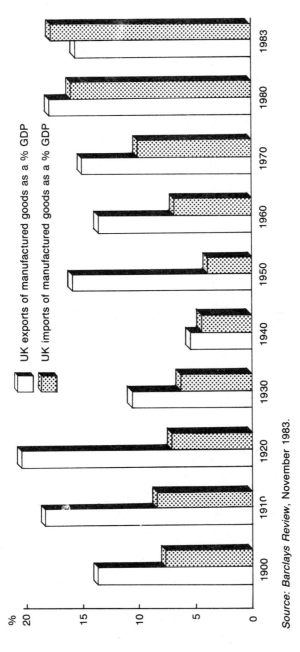

UK exports of manufactured goods as a % GDP

UK imports of manufactured goods as a % GDP

Source: Barclays Review, November 1983.

Appendix 4 Trends in Manufactured Goods

Appendix 5 Import Penetration Figures

	Exports (f.o.b.) CGJP £ (million)	Imports (f.o.b.) CGGL £ (million)	Visible balance HCHL £ (million)
1946	960	1 063	−103
1947	1 180	1 541	−361
1948	1 639	1 790	−151
1949	1 863	2 000	−137
1950	2 261	2 312	−51
1951	2 735	3 424	−689
1952	2 769	3 048	−279
1953	2 683	2 927	−244
1954	2 785	2 989	−204
1955	3 073	3 386	−313
1956	3 377	3 324	53
1957	3 509	3 538	−29
1958	3 406	3 377	29
1959	3 527	3 642	−115
1960	3 737	4 138	−401
1961	3 903	4 043	−140
1962	4 003	4 103	−100
1963	4 331	4 450	−119
1964	4 568	5 111	−543
1965	4 913	5 173	−260
1966	5 276	5 384	−108
1967	5 241	5 840	−599
1968	6 433	7 145	−712
1969	7 269	7 478	−209
1970	8 150	8 184	−34
1971	9 043	8 853	190
1972	9 347	10 185	−838
1973	11 937	14 523	−2 586
1974	16 394	21 745	−5 351
1975	19 330	22 663	−3 333
1976	25 191	29 120	−3 929
1977	31 725	34 012	−2 287
1978	35 063	36 605	−1 542
1979	40 687	44 136	−3 449
1980	47 422	46 061	1 361
1981	50 977	47 617	3 360
1982	55 565	53 234	2 331
1983	50 778	61 611	−10 833
1984	70 367	74 751	−4 384
1985	78 111	80 289	−2 178
1986	72 843	81 306	−8 463

Source: CSO (1988) *Economic Trends.*

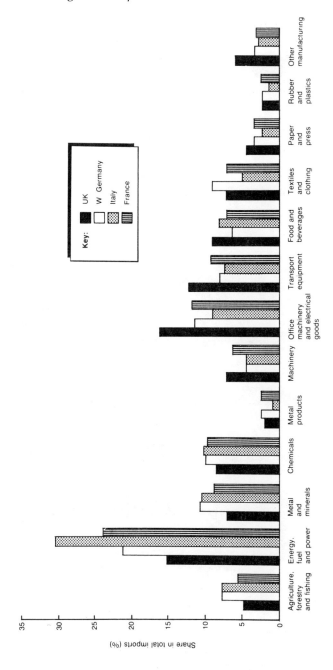

Source: NEDC (1987) *British Industrial Performance.*

Note: French data is for 1985.

Appendix 6 Comparison of Imports to the UK, W. Germany, Italy and France

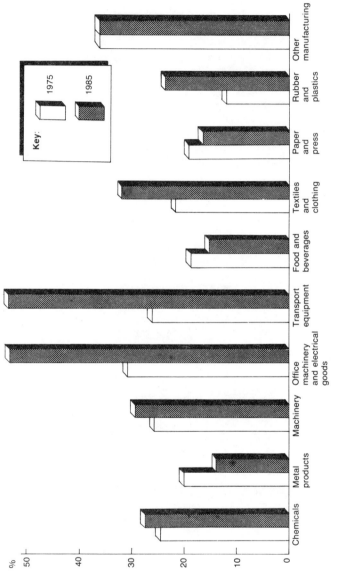

Source: NEDC (1987) *British Industrial Performance.*

Appendix 7 Imports as a Percentage of Sales

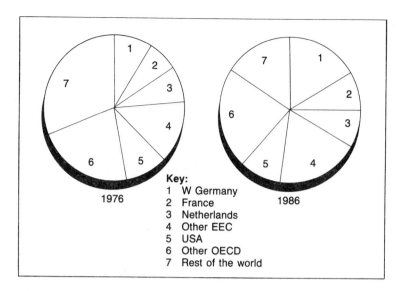

Key:
1 W Germany
2 France
3 Netherlands
4 Other EEC
5 USA
6 Other OECD
7 Rest of the world

Source: NEDC (1987) *British Industrial Performance.*

Appendix 8 UK Import Markets: Percentage of Total Value

References

Buckley, P.J., Pass, C.L. and Prescott, K. (1988) 'Measures of international competitiveness: a critical survey', *Journal of Marketing Management*, vol. 4, no. 2.

Central Statistical Office (1988) *Economic Trends.*

Commission of European Communities (1983) The EEC Telecom Industry, *Competition, Concentration and Competitiveness,* Luxembourg Office for Official Publications of the European Communities.

Connell, D. (1979) *The UK's Performance in Export Markets: Some Evidence from International Trade Data,* NEDO, Discussion Paper 6.

Drucker, P. (1954) *The Practice of Management,* Harper and Row.

G. El D.M. Morsey (1986) *Competitive Marketing Strategy: A Study of Competitive Performance in the British Car Market,* Unpublished Ph.D Thesis, University of Strathclyde, November.

Francis, A. (1986) *The Concept of Competitiveness,* ESRC Working Paper.

Francis, A. (1987) 'The competitiveness of British industry', *ESRC Newsletter,* vol. 58, September.

Francis, A. and Winstanley, D. (1988) 'Managing new product develop-
ment: some alternative ways to organise the work of technical
specialists', *Journal of Marketing Management*, Winter, vol. 4, no. 2, pp.
149–260.
Galbraith, J.K. (1958) *The Affluent Society*, Houghton Mifflin.
Goldsmith, W. and Clutterbuck, D. (1984) *The Winning Streak: Britain's
Top Companies Reveal Their Formulas for Success*, Weidenfeld & Nicolson.
Harrod, R. (1967) 'Assessing the trade returns', *Economic Journal*,
September.
Harvey-Jones, J. (1986) *Does industry matter?* The Dimbleby Lecture, *The
Listener*, April.
HMSO (1985) Report from the Select Committee of the House of Lords
on Overseas Trade (the *Aldington Report*), HL238.
Hooley, G.J., Lynch, J.E. and West, C.J. (1984) *Marketing in the UK: A
Survey of Current Practices and Performance*, The Institute of Marketing.
Karel, W., Williams, J. and Thomas, D. (1983) *Why Are The British Bad
at Manufacturing?* Routledge & Kegan Paul.
Krugman, P.R. and Hatsopoulos, G.N. (1987) 'The problem of US com-
petitiveness in manufacturing', *New England Economic Review*, Federal
Reserve Bank of Boston, January–February.
Levitt, T. (1960) 'Marketing myopia', *Harvard Business Review*.
Levitt, T. (1983) *The Marketing Imagination*, The Free Press.
Macmillan Dictionary of Marketing and Advertising (1984), Macmillan.
NEDO (1965) *Imported Manufactures, An Enquiry into Competitiveness*,
NEDO.
NEDO (1977) *International Price Competitiveness, Non-price Factors and Export
Performance*, NEDO.
Packard, V. (1957) *The Hidden Persuaders*, David McKay Co.
Packard, V. (1960) *The Waste Makers*, David McKay Co.
Peters, T.J. and Waterman, R.H. (1982) *In Search of Excellence*, Harper
& Row.
Pollard, S. (1980) *The Development of the British Economy 1919–1980* (3rd
edn), Edward Arnold.
Porter, M. (1980) *Competitive Strategy*, Free Press.
Prowse, M. (1985) 'Why services may be no substitute for manufactur-
ing', *Financial Times*, 25 October.
Saunders, J. (1988) 'The ESRC Competitiveness Initiative', *Journal of
Marketing Management*, Winter, vol. 4, no. 2, pp. 103–6.
Scibberas, E. (1986) 'Indicators of technical intensity and international
competitiveness: a case for supplementing quantitative data with
qualitative studies in research', *Research and Development Management*,
vol. 16, no. 1.
Thirwall, A.P. (1982) *Balance of Payments Theory and the United Kingdom
Experience*, Macmillan.

2

The Sources of Competitiveness

2.1 Introduction

In the preceding chapter it soon became apparent that over the last 150 years there has been an almost continuous decline in the United Kingdom's share of world trade. Given that Britain spawned the Industrial Revolution and was once the 'workshop of the world', accounting for over 40 per cent of all world trade (by definition 50 per cent is the maximum any single country can achieve), it is unsurprising that her share should contract as other nations industrialised and began to compete with her. Of course, such competition leads to an increase in world trade, which in real terms is now orders of magnitude greater than it was in the nineteenth century; thus, while the UK *share* is of interest, what matter most are the absolute value and the composition and net balance of our international trade. It is changes in the latter — composition and balance — which underlie the growing concern with the continuing decline in the UK's competitiveness in manufactures, and which comprise the visible element in our trade balance and have been in deficit for the last 15 years (with the exception of the years 1980–2).

In order to understand the factors underlying this loss of competitiveness — an essential prerequisite to any prognosis for remedial action — it is necessary first to understand the nature and sources of competition, and this is the main objective of this chapter. Given that the primary purpose of an economy is to maximise the satisfaction obtained from the utilisation of the scarce resources available to it, it soon becomes evident that task specialisation and the division of labour offer significant increases in productivity. However, task specialisation and the division of labour can only be pursued effectively if there exists a market in which surpluses can be exchanged. Thus 'marketing' and the exchange which results are the source of added value which enhances satisfaction and so enables economies to achieve their basic purpose.

In the early stages of economic development the progress and growth of communities is severely limited by the supply of resources immediately available to them, but with the development of transportation it becomes possible to expand the geographical trading area and so extend the benefits of specialisation to embrace areas with quite different natural factor advantages. International trade is the result, and the theory of comparative advantage emerges to explain why such trade is to the benefit of all the participants. These topics provide the initial focus of the chapter.

At this stage of economic development there was comparatively little competition as we know it today for the simple reason that demand was growing rapidly and far exceeded the available supply, save for some essential goods and services. However, with industrialisation this imbalance began to change, leading to increased competition and the sort of competitive markets with which we are familiar today. The growth of competition and its implications for international trade comprise the second part of the chapter.

2.2   Theories of International Trade

Ever since Adam Smith published *The Wealth of Nations* in 1776, the nature and purposes of international trade have been a major preoccupation of economic theorists. Prior to Smith, attitudes to international trade were dominated by the theories of the *mercantilists* who maintained that for a country to become rich and powerful it had to export more than it imported leading to an inflow of bullion. Given that all nations cannot simultaneously achieve an export surplus and that, at least in the short term, the amount of gold and silver is fixed, then clearly one nation can benefit only at the expense of another. Thus, while governments would encourage exports and discourage imports such policies are doomed to failure in the long term as a net inflow of gold arising from an export surplus would increase the money supply and lead to a rise in prices. Conversely, with countries in deficit, prices would fall so that the terms of trade between the two countries would move in favour of the deficit country and against the surplus country. As such, mercantilist policies were seen as carrying the seeds of their own destruction, and Smith started from the simple proposition that for international trade to flourish all the participants must gain.

According to Smith, such an outcome would result if countries concentrated on producing those goods in which they enjoyed an *absolute advantage* over other countries, and then exported their surpluses in exchange for the surpluses of other countries which enjoyed an absolute advantage over them. By extending the principle of task specialisation to the international arena, resources such as land, labour and capital will be used to maximum effect, thus achieving a greater output of the commodities concerned, to the mutual benefit of the trading partners. Accordingly, Smith and the school of classical economists who followed him advocated a *laissez-faire* approach to free trade, in direct contrast to the strictly controlled approaches advocated by the mercantilists.

However, Smith's theory assumed that every trading country would enjoy an absolute cost advantage for at least one product which it would be able to trade internationally; this raises the question of what advantage would accrue to the country with no absolute advantage. To address this issue, David Ricardo proposed his theory of *comparative advantage* — one of the first purely theoretical explanations developed in the discipline of economics. Like many such theories it suffers from its 'static' nature, in that in order to identify the critical factors and their interactions, one has to exclude many real-world complications from the analysis by the simple expedient of assuming that they don't exist. Hence, the theory of comparative advantage rests on the simplifying assumptions that:

- there are only two nations, two goods and a single factor (labour);
- free trade exists;
- there is perfect mobility of labour within each nation, but none between the two nations;

- there are no economies of scale;
- there are no transportation costs;
- there is no technological change.

This is hardly a typical representation of the world as we know it, and as such the source of the major criticisms levelled against the theory. For example, Ricardo's theory is, in essence, one of labour productivity, but it assumes that in a competitive market a single factor price (wages) would prevail when the reality is that they vary with skill and between industries. Notwithstanding these practical deficiencies, Ricardo's contribution was to demonstrate that absolute advantage was not a necessary condition for two countries to engage in international trade to their mutual benefit. Rather, he showed that if a country specialised in the production and export of those goods in which its absolute disadvantage was smallest (i.e. its source of comparative advantage) and imported those goods in which its absolute disadvantage was greatest, then it would increase its output overall.

Given that the concept of comparative advantage is both intuitively and logically appealing, subsequent generations of theoreticians have devoted their energies to developing more comprehensive multifactor explanations, of which the best known is the so-called Heckscher–Ohlin Theorem. The essence of this theorem is to explain the pattern of international trade in terms of factor abundance, such that countries will export those goods whose production utilises most intensively those factors in scarcest supply. Provided one accepts the conditions/assumptions of the theorists then the Heckscher–Ohlin approach constitutes a satisfactory explanation of international trade. Sufficient to say (and for reasons beyond the scope of this book but amply documented elsewhere), the conditions and assumptions define a static framework and so, like Ricardo, fail to capture the dynamic reality.

In his survey based upon a wide-ranging literature review Abdel-Mohsen (1986) summarises the key assumptions of Heckscher–Ohlin as follows:

1. Technology is static and countries have equal access to technical know-how.
2. Rankings of commodities according to factor intensities of

production are identical across countries, irrespective of
variations in factor price.

3. Both types of countries are incompletely specialised and
   continue to produce both products in international
   equilibrium.
4. Industries operate in a climate of perfect competition and
   free trade.
5. Consumer preferences are identical across countries, and
   are determined solely by relative prices.
6. Governments do not interfere with free trade through
   tariffs, quotas, taxes or other regulations.

As noted, hardly a convincing set of real-world assumptions, and
Abdel-Mohsen continues to cite the leading criticisms of the comparative advantage approaches as being:

1. The Ricardian and Heckscher–Ohlin models involve
   reducing the world economy to distinct pairs of countries
   exchanging distinct pairs of commodities.
2. Neoclassicists have usually chosen food and clothing (the
   staple commodities of international trade of their time) as
   their typical commodities and have assumed that price
   alone determines consumer preference.
3. Both are static models and fail to deal with dynamic issues
   concerning the determinants of change in comparative
   advantage over time.
4. The trade effects of change in demand patterns associated
   with economic growth and development are not treated
   within the Heckscher–Ohlin theory. Similarly, the impact
   of technological innovation on comparative advantage is
   ignored through the assumption of identical international
   production functions and the failure to discuss the
   introduction of new products or changes in production
   over time.

This failure to capture the essential nature of competitive
advantage was highlighted by the findings of a survey by Leontief
(1954) in which he set out to determine whether, as Heckscher–
Ohlin would have predicted, the USA's comparative advantage
in international trade in manufactured goods was attributable to
the country's relative abundance of capital over labour. His con-

MOUNT PLEASANT LIBRARY
TEL. 051 207 3581 Ext. 3701

clusion showed that the opposite was true: US imports were more capital intensive than her exports, a result characterised as the Leontief paradox and confirmed in numerous studies, particularly (and most recently) in Rothwell's (1981, 1983) analyses of competitiveness in the textile and agricultural machinery industries.

On the grounds that factor-proportions analysis is unable to explain intra-regional trade (within a region, factor proportions are, by definition, homogeneous), Linder concluded that other, albeit unidentified, variables were more important. In arriving at this conclusion, he also articulated the important alternative hypothesis that a country cannot achieve export competitiveness in any manufactured items which have not first catered for domestic demands. While this proposition appears eminently sensible — if not tautological, once stated — it must be recognised that it is in complete contradiction to the central prediction in the Heckscher–Ohlin model. Of course, Heckscher–Ohlin, like most theorists, were allowing themselves the luxury of the clean-sheet-of-paper approach: what would you do with currently available knowledge if you were to establish economies from scratch and maximise their collective outputs by stipulating what should be produced and exchanged by whom? But national economies and concepts of independence and self-sufficiency antedated the search for explanations concerning variants in the effectiveness of those economies in improving the welfare of their citizens. Thus, the concern of the politicians and policy-makers must be to interpret the theory in terms of the insights it can bring to improving what *is* rather than to regard it as an inviolate statement of what *must be*. Accordingly, Linder's pragmatic observation should be combined with the predictions of the factor-proportions theorists to evolve at least two working guidelines:

- The sooner firms seek to trade internationally, the sooner they will achieve increased sales and the benefits associated with economies of scale.
- Exports should be directed to countries whose income level is roughly equal to that of the exporting country.

But much still remains to be explained. Two further approaches which seek to do this by admitting additional variables to the analysis are the *technology-gap* and *product-life-cycle* theories.

The first of these theories (technology gap) is associated

primarily with the work of Michael Posner (1961) who pointed out that 'by technical changes and developments that influence some industries and not others, because particular technical changes originate in one country, comparative cost differences may induce trade in particular goods during the lapse of time taken for the rest of the world to imitate one country's innovation.' The time lag in countries adopting another's innovation is seen as comprising three components. First, there is the time taken for the international transmission of the necessary technical knowledge (the 'foreign reaction lag'), a factor which has reduced progressively in recent years to the point where it is now estimated that knowledge of a new technology is fully diffused worldwide within a period of 18 months. Second, there is the 'domestic reaction lag' which defines the time taken for producers in other countries to adopt the new technology. Third, there is the time required to master the new technique (the learning process).

With regard to the domestic reaction lag and the effort which a foreign producer would be prepared to invest in mastering a new technique, it is clear that this will depend very largely upon perceptions of the size and scope of the market opportunity opened up by the new technology. As Rogers (1962) has pointed out, speed of adoption is a function of a variety of factors which he has labelled relative advantage, complexity, compatibility, communicability and divisibility — in other words, the larger the benefit offered, the easier it is to understand that benefit, the less disruption it will cause to current ways of doing things, and the more quickly users will switch to the innovation. Effective marketing is a critical factor whatever the situation.

If the benefits offered by an innovation are large and immediate then consumers will begin to switch their purchasing power in its favour, as soon as it becomes available. However, failure to prepare production and adequate finance up to the required levels of demand will result in unsatisfied customers looking for other potential suppliers, while failure to develop adequate channels of distribution, and to promote and service the product, will also provide opportunities for imitators to cash in on the innovator's breakthrough. Conversely, if the innovation's benefits are not so immediately apparent, and if use of this innovation requires the adopter to make significant changes in his current behaviour, then take-up is likely to be slow, and competition will bide its time to see which way the market will jump. Under such circumstances, innovators frequently expend all their resources on developing awareness and interest in a potential market only to see a 'fast second' capitalise on their market development efforts. In such cases, effective marketing will enable the innovator to focus his limited launch resources on the most receptive market segments and so increase the likelihood of being able to keep in front of predatory imitators. (See Baker 1983 for a full discussion of this issue.)

Although Posner himself did not test his theory empirically he inspired numerous others to do so. Foremost among these was Freeman (1963) whose analysis of the plastics industries in advanced countries showed that location of production and per capita exports were functions of technical progress as measured by research expenditures, patents and innovation. In turn, Freeman set up the Science Policy Research Unit at Sussex University whose members have been the source of a continuous flow of studies exploring the contribution of technology to competitiveness and economic growth, and, in the process (Project SAPPHO 1974), were among the first to isolate marketing as a critical success factor.

Other studies, particularly in the USA, led Walker (1979) to criticise the technology-gap theory on the grounds that it was unable to predict the timing and direction of production transfer from innovator to imitator countries and so prompted Ray Vernon (1966) and his colleagues at the Harvard Business School to develop a detailed product-life-cycle explanation of international trade.

Vernon's starting point seems to be Linder's observation that international trade develops from the existence of a product within a domestic market, from which it will diffuse to other international markets. If, therefore, comparative advantage depends largely upon technological sophistication, then it would seem reasonable to expect trade to flow from more-advanced to less-advanced economies. Thus, Vernon argued that: 'the United States market consists of consumers with an average income which is higher than that in any other national market — twice as high as that of Western Europe, for instance; wherever there was a chance to offer a new product responsive to wants at high levels of income, this chance would presumably first be apparent to someone in a position to observe the United States' markets'. Implicit in this quotation is the view that more affluent customers are better able to assume the risks associated with innovation when costs are high (no economies of scale) and performance outcomes less certain. Based upon this assumption, it becomes possible to extrapolate from the concept of the product life cycle because it relates a specific product to the concept of an international product life cycle as an explanation of international trade patterns.

The product-life-cycle concept is believed to be one of the most important analytical frameworks in the marketing discipline. While it is not without its critics who have mistaken its purpose — a generalised representation of the shape of the cumulative sales of a product over time from introduction (birth) to withdrawal (death) — and attempted to use it as a predictive device, the PLC concept is a fundamental statement about the inevitability of change, which is both the catalyst for and the consequence of competition. The PLC is depicted graphically in Figure 2.1 and proposes that, following its launch, a new pro-

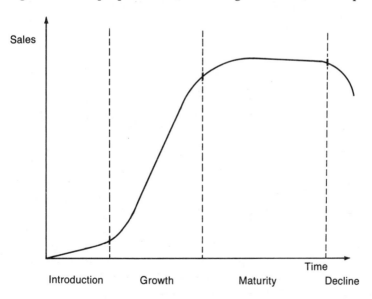

Figure 2.1 The Product Life Cycle

duct (innovation) will initially make slow progress in the market place as potential users learn of its existence, are persuaded of its benefits and have the opportunity to acquire a supply of it. As the introductory phase progresses, the first buyers or innovators will help to increase awareness of the innovation and so stimulate wider interest, whilst experience and scale effects will allow the producer to offer an improved product and, if he wishes, reduce the offer price. Collectively, these factors will induce a rapid acceleration in sales and will initiate the Growth phase (the *contagion* or *bandwagon* effect). Ultimately, however, there is a limit to the consumption of everything so that, as the market becomes saturated, sales will eventually settle down into equilibrium in the Mature phase. But every innovation contains within itself the seeds of its own destruction for, by raising the expectations of consumers, it creates a desire for yet further improvement. Inevitably a further innovation will be introduced and will begin to compete with the old innovation so that as its sales slowly grow those of the established product will begin to decline slowly. Conventionally, one does not continue the PLC curve to its logical conclusion but it requires little imagination to perceive that if one were to do so one would finish up with a virtually symmetrical curve approximating that of a normal distribution.

The concept of the life cycle is also central to the work of Hirsch whose *Location of Industry and International Competitiveness* was published in 1967 (the year after Vernon's work). In this book, Hirsch presents the 'characteristics of the product cycle' as depicted in Table 2.1. While differing in detail from more conventional representations of the stages associated with the PLC, the table summarises well the changes which will occur as a product progresses through its life cycle and so emphasises the dynamic nature of the process absent from the Ricardian and Heckscher—Ohlin models. This contrast is summarised in Table 2.2, in which Louis Wells (a colleague of Vernon's) compares the Heckscher—Ohlin and PLC approaches. As noted above, the early stage is characterised by uncertain demand and rapid changes in the technology as producers gain experience in use and respond to user needs. Competition will be based largely on non-price factors with few, if any, competitors offering substitute products. As the product begins to move into the growth stage

Table 2.1 Characteristics of the Product Life Cycle

| | *Cycle Phase* | | |
	Early	*Growth*	*Mature*
Technology	Short runs, rapidly changing techniques, dependence on external economies.	Mass production methods gradually introduced. Variations in techniques still frequent.	Long run and stable process. Few innovations of importance.
Capital intensity	Low.	High, due to high obsolescence rate.	High, due to quantity of specialised equipment.
Industry structure	Entry is 'know-how' determined. Numerous firms.	Growing number of firms. Many casualties and mergers. Growing integration.	Market position and financial resources affect entry. Number of firms declining.
Critical human inputs	Scientific and engineering.	Management.	Unskilled labour, semi-skilled labour.
Demand structure	Sellers' market. Performance and price of substitutes determine buyers' expectations.	Individual producers face growing price elasticity. Competition reducing prices. Product information spreading.	Buyers' market. Information easily available.

Source: Hirsch (1967), p. 23.

its performance characteristics/specification become established and the need to produce on a larger scale to meet the growing demand results in substantial capital investment, particularly as new firms seek to exploit the proven market opportunity. Growth

Table 2.2　Differences Between Ohlin and the Product Life Cycle Theory

Heckscher—Ohlin	*Product Life Cycle*
(1) Identical production functions in all countries for each commodity or differences due only to neutral efficiency differential.	(1) Production function changes with time: early in the life of the product it is more labour and skill intensive than later.
(2) Linear, homogeneous production functions with diminishing marginal productivity for each factor.	(2) Increasing returns to scale.
(3) Non-reversibility of factor intensities.	(3) Reversibility not excluded. Some authors assume essentially identical production functions in all countries in the late phase.
(4) Identical consumption patterns in all countries at any given set of international prices, i.e. all commodities are consumed in same proportions regardless of income level.	(4) Consumption patterns differ by income levels. Some goods account for a higher proportion of consumption for countries at higher level of income. Such products are called 'high-income' products.
(5) Perfect market, free trade and no transportation costs.	(5) The transmission of knowledge across international boundaries is assumed to have a cost. Inside a country, the transmission of knowledge between firm and market is assumed to have a cost. Trade barriers and transportation costs are allowed to exist.
(6) International immobility of productive factors.	(6) Capital is assumed by many authors to be at least partially mobile.
(7) Qualitatively identical production factors.	(7) No assumption.
(8) Full employment, static.	(8) No assumption on employment dynamic.

Source: Wells (1984), p. 16.

accelerates as much from supply-push as from demand-pull and will prompt producers to widen the original, geographically bounded domestic market through international trade.

Initially, most producers will wish to limit their risk exposure and will follow an export strategy. However, as Vernon points out, depending upon the attractiveness of the market, the nature of tariff barriers, the costs and behaviour of competition, transportation etc., domestic producers may decide to invest abroad. By the mature phase the technology and its associated production processes have become well known, and direct foreign investment by the innovator will become essential as competition will now have a strong price dimension and cost reduction has become imperative. Thus, the original producer will seek to site his production facilities in locations which enjoy a comparative advantage in terms of factor inputs; this may even result in the closure of production facilities in the country which first initiated the cycle. At this point the various theories come together and, as Hirsch (1967) indicates, should be seen as complementary rather than competing theories in much the same way as a series of snapshots (static) can be combined to give a moving picture (dynamic) of change as it occurs.

Based upon his extensive review of the empirical evidence contained in the published work of researchers who have explored the application of the technology-gap and life-cycle theories Abdel-Mohsen (1986) concludes that:

1. It is now widely recognised that technological superiority provides a country with competitive advantages in international trade and investment. But a given technological innovation diffuses abroad sooner or later, eliminating the advantage of the innovator. Thus, international migration of new technologies, along with their creation, forms the foundation of the dynamic theory of competitive advantage.

2. The dynamic process of the product life cycle suggests that policy planners and manufacturers in the advanced countries might be able to anticipate the decline of their competitive strength in products or industries which are approaching the mature phase of the cycle.

3. Finally, the effect of technology and product life cycle theories is to add a further dimension to the complexity of competitiveness. Emphasis is now given to the quality of the saleable

article. Commercial rivalry takes a non-price form. Competitiveness comes to mean product as well as price competitiveness. This type of competitiveness may be no less dynamic than the more conventional form of price rivalry — non-price rivalry can be dynamic, dog-eat-dog affairs. Furthermore, it is likely to have more relevance to the rate of technological progress than competitiveness based on price.

From the above excerpt it is clear that the exchange process is the mechanism through which satisfaction gained from the consumption of scarce resources will be maximised — in other words *exchange* adds value. This being so, it makes sense that individuals, families, firms and nations should concentrate their efforts on producing those things which they can produce 'better' (more cost effectively) than others and they should exchange their surpluses with one another. Unfortunately, abilities and resources (supply creation potential) are not distributed in such a way that if everyone followed this policy the resulting output would match, even crudely, the needs and wants of the producers in their capacities as consumers. Nevertheless, many abilities and resources *can* be put to multiple uses; thus, if we are to maximise aggregate satisfaction, we need an allocative mechanism which ensures that producers can decide which goods and services will yield them the best return on their efforts. Of course, we have such a mechanism — the market — and a medium of exchange (money) which enables us to establish the value of one output to any other output. But we do not possess perfect information, and even if we did it is highly probable that different individuals would interpret the facts differently. As a result, the market allocative system is imperfect and it frequently operates heuristically, on a basis of trial and error, giving rise to what we generally refer to as 'competition'. This competition is now truly global in nature, with many more 'players' than a century ago when Britain was a major world exporter of manufactures and importer of raw materials and foodstuffs. We still need raw materials and foodstuffs but, as a result of economic development, many of our traditional markets are now denied us and, in some cases, have become our competitors. Clearly, if we wish to arrest the decline chronicled in Chapter 1, and recognising the logic of participating in international trade as established in the preceding pages, then it follows that we must understand more fully what constitutes the basis of competition; it is to this we turn in the second part of this chapter.

2.3 Theories of Competition

In our discussion of theories of international trade we observed that the main deficiencies of the Ricardian and Heckscher–Ohlin concepts of comparative advantage were that they were static and were founded on a series of assumptions which bore little relation to the real world. But identification of these deficiencies led others to seek more powerful and realistic explanations of value to policy planners and decision-makers. Much the same evolution can be detected in the development of theories of competition. In Baker (1985) these theories are described as follows:

> In essence the nature of competition and of market structure is the outcome of the interaction between supply and demand. As indicated above, it is normal to define two limiting conditions — monopoly and pure competition — and to categorise intermediate forms of competition as 'imperfect'. What, then, are the salient characteristics of these states? Before addressing this issue it is necessary to introduce the concept of demand elasticity, for it is this factor which is usually used as the basic indicator of the nature of competition.
>
> Under normal conditions most people anticipate that an increase in the price of a good will result in a decline in the amount demanded, while conversely any fall in price should be accompanied by an increase in the quantity demanded. In simple terms, elasticity is a measure of the degree to which a change in price will result in a change in demand. Where a very small change in price is accompanied by a major change in demand, we say that that product has a high elasticity of demand. Conversely, even where significant price changes have only a limited impact upon the quantity demanded, we say that that product has a low elasticity of demand. Thus, in order to determine the elasticity of demand for the given good, we need to measure the magnitude of changes in the quantity demanded in relation to changes in the unit price. Such information is termed a *demand schedule* and is frequently represented graphically, as in Figure 2.2, from which it can be seen that infinitely elastic demand is represented by a horizontal line, infinitely inelastic demand by a vertical line, while varying degrees of elasticity are represented by the angle assumed by the demand curve.
>
> In terms of basic competitive states, demand under pure competition is usually represented as being highly — if not infinitely — elastic,

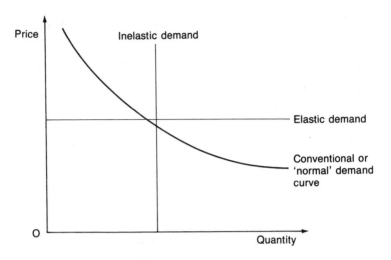

Figure 2.2 Demand Curves

while under monopoly conditions demand is considered highly inelastic. However, for a state of pure competition or monopoly to exist certain conditions must be satisfied.

In the case of pure competition, three basic conditions must be satisfied: namely, a large number of producers, homogeneous output, and freedom of entry. In fact, when talking of a large number of firms it would be more accurate to speak of low levels of concentration, for the basic condition which we are seeking to define is one in which decisions by any single firm have little or no effect upon the output of the industry as a whole. As we have noted earlier, homogeneity in a product depends upon the perception of a prospective buyer. Only in the case of commodities and raw materials is it usual to find agreement that the output of two different producers which meets a given specification can, in fact, be treated as identical products. The third condition for the existence of pure competition is freedom of entry, by which we mean that there are no barriers or artificial restrictions to prevent any individual or firm from setting up in business to produce supplies of the product in question.

It should be noted that pure competition is not synonymous with perfect competition, for the former describes only the competitive state between suppliers, while the latter makes further assumptions about conditions in the market. Essentially, these assumptions are that all buyers and sellers have perfect knowledge of the activities of one another, that there are no transportation costs and that there is perfect mobility of factors of production between industries. Under these conditions the market determines the price of a product and so, effectively, the firm has no control over its destiny whatsoever.

The polar extreme to a situation of perfect competition is one of pure monopoly. By definition, a monopolist is the sole supplier of a particular product or service, with the result that firm and industry are synonymous. In economic theory a pure monopolist has no competition at all; clearly such a position cannot exist, for it presumes that the monopolist commands all of a consumer's income. For practical purposes we consider that a state of monopoly exists when there is no close substitute for the monopolist's output. Applying the concept of concentration, we see that a monopolist would have a concentration ratio of 100 per cent. Because the monopolist does not face direct competition from other suppliers, as is the case under conditions of perfect competition, it is frequently assumed that he has no incentive to maximise his efficiency.

Clearly, under conditions of perfect competition, the producer must maximise his efficiency, for if he does not his costs will rise above those of his rivals and he will be unable to recoup these higher costs through increased prices. In the long run, therefore, the inefficient producer, under conditions of perfect competition, will be forced out of business.

From the foregoing descriptions it is clear that conditions of perfect competition and pure monopoly are exceptions rather than the rule: they are the limiting conditions. Under both sets of conditions the seller reacts solely to external environmental forces. However, in intermediate states between the two extremes the factor which really distinguishes imperfect competition is that the firm has to take account not only of the external environment within which it must operate, but also of the action of other suppliers in the market-place. The need, under conditions of imperfect competition, for firms to take into account the actions of their immediate competitors makes for a much more complex situation, and one demanding a far higher level of managerial skill. Under conditions of imperfect competition sellers are mutually interdependent, and so must allow for each other's actions when formulating their plans.

As noted earlier when discussing different managerial orientations during this present century, the growth of imperfect competition is of relatively recent origin. In fact, it was not until the early 1930s that Edward Chamberlin and Joan Robinson first put forward their theories on the subject. In time, therefore, the proposal of a theory of imperfect competition coincided with a change from the production to the sales management orientation and the need for companies to compete with one another along dimensions other than cost and price.

Theories of imperfect competition frequently invite an analogy with games in which choices of courses of action are limited not only by the rules of the game but also by the actions of one's competitors.

Thus we find that the study of competition places increasing emphasis upon the strategic choices made by participating firms and the impact which these have upon both the fortunes of their competitors and market structure. In making such choices, firms have to operate within the environmental constraints — political, legal and social — common to them all. Thus, in order to develop a distinctive and, it is hoped, successful strategy they have found it beneficial to give much closer attention to microeconomic aspects of supply and demand — especially the latter.

Microeconomic aspects of supply are concerned with the behaviour of the firm — a subject which would fill several chapters, if not books. In economics, the 'theory of the firm' adopts a number of simplifying assumptions in order to provide a benchmark against which to compare real-world behaviour. *Inter alia*, these include the assumption that the individual entrepreneur is the owner of the firm and that his prime objective is to maximise money profits. In reality, most firms have multiple owners, are professionally managed and pursue policies which Simon and March (1959) have defined as 'satisfying' rather than seeking to maximise. As Baker has noted (ibid. 1985): 'The reasons why the unbridled pursuit of profit should not be the sole objective of management is apparent in the role of profit itself. Profit is generally regarded as the reward for the assumption of risk and on the whole it is accepted that the greater the risk, the greater should be the reward. It is also accepted that risk is usually measured in terms of the likelihood of loss. Accordingly professional management tends to try and balance its activities in such a manner so as not to put the whole corporation at risk. Clearly by doing so it forgoes the possibility of maximising profits. It also avoids the possibility of maximising losses!' Thus most firms satisfice in the sense that they see survival as the primary objective and growth as the second.

In order both to survive and grow, firms will also tend to take the line of least resistance by seeking to operate in those markets with the largest and most stable demand. As noted previously, theories of competition reflect the reality of their times so that Adam Smith's two basic states — full and free competition and pure monopoly (albeit on a strictly local basis) — mirrored the situation in an economy which had undergone an agricultural revolution and was on the verge of an industrial revolution. With the developments in transportation and communication which accompanied the industrial revolution, manufacturers gained access to much larger markets. However, the choice to compete in the mass markets for basic goods and services was largely due to the fact that average disposable incomes were low and most expenditure was concentrated on such basic goods. To succeed in such markets with large unsatisfied demands and low disposable income the emphasis was upon increasing supply and reducing costs and prices — objectives most readily achieved by concentrating upon product standardisation and manufacturing efficiencies. This era, which spanned the nineteenth century, probably came to an end in 1921 in the USA and has been characterised as a production orientation.

We can propose such a precise date for the transition from a production to a new 'sales' orientation because Alfred Sloan tells us in *My Years at General Motors* (1963) that it was in the summer of 1921 that the product planning committee at GM was looking for a strategy to challenge the dominance of Ford, who had more than a 60 per cent share of the US automobile market. Ford's preeminence was founded upon the single-minded pursuit of economies of scale through a policy of complete product standardisation. As a result, Ford could make and sell cars for less than anyone else and, for those who believe that consumers buy solely on the basis of price, his market leadership must have seemed unassailable. But, as the boys at GM recognised, most demand curves slope downwards from left to right, which implies that while sales will increase as prices fall, some people are able and willing to pay more than the going market price. Obviously if you pay more you expect more for your money but, given that Ford's Model T was such a basic car, it didn't take a great deal of imagination to see how to improve upon it through *a policy of product differentiation*. Thus GM decided to build a range of models catering for people with different levels of disposable income. However, differentiated products have to be promoted and sold, and it was the addition of product and selling efforts alongside the economists' traditional preoccupation with price and output that resulted in the need for a radical restructuring in the theory of the firm and gave rise to Joan Robinson's and Edward Chamberlin's theories of imperfect competition.

A particular attraction of a policy of product differentiation is that if one can successfully position one's product in the consumer's mind as distinctive from all other products in that category, and to be preferred because of this distinctiveness, then one has a monopoly or consumer franchise, and so can exercise a degree of control over the market rather than being controlled by it. However, as consumers become more affluent and sophisticated, the likelihood that producers will be able to predetermine the precise nature of demand decreases, and it becomes necessary to modify the production/sales orientation and switch from 'selling what we can make' to 'making what we can sell'. The latter, *marketing orientation*, rests on the simple proposition that the 'satisfaction' which economies are seeking to maximise is the satisfaction of the ordinary consumer, and the obvious way of achieving this is to ask consumers what they want and then organise production and sales to see that they get it. While the concept is simple, the execution is less so. That said, a central theme of this book is that effective marketing is a necessary condition for competitive success and one to which we return in the succeeding chapters. However, before doing so it will be helpful to examine how product differentiation has resulted in competition, taking on board a whole range of non-price factors in addition to the price element which the conventional wisdom sees as the central factor in choice and buying decisions.

2.4   Price versus Non-price Factors

When products are truly undifferentiated rationality demands that one buy the one with the lowest price as this clearly offers greater value than any product with a higher price. But, with the exception of basic commodities and products manufactured to a strict specification (cement, steel, etc.), users are likely to perceive differences between different suppliers even though, in reality, their outputs are physically identical. As a result, consumers infer that higher prices imply higher quality, albeit that they are unable to identify precisely what this is. Indeed, paying a higher price can be seen as a form of risk reduction even in major capital investment decisions. To a great extent this essentially non-rational behaviour is due to the conflict between economic theory, which proposes that one should always pay the lowest price because this reflects the most efficient producer, and our experience that 'you get what you pay for'. This latter, deeply ingrained, attitude is the consequence of centuries of buying experience which have proved that, while objects may appear identical, their performance varies enormously, and the more complex the product, the more likely this is to be the case. Thus users have always looked for cues to enable them to differentiate between products and now, with product differentiation as the basic competitive strategy, producers have obliged by providing specific information on factors which distinguish their product and may account for differences in price. From the manufacturer's point of view non-price competition is to be preferred for the simple reason that it offers some degree of control over the market, whereas price competition will result in the elimination of smaller, less efficient producers and the erosion of profit margins for the larger, more efficient producers.

The most important and effective form of non-price competition is product differentiation, with the result that product policy has become the key factor in marketing-mix decisions. Indeed, Chamberlin himself, in articulating his theory, stated that 'the admission of the product as a variable not only adds to the picture an alternative area in which competition may in fact be quite active; it does much more than this, it supplies a powerful new force working against price competition.'

Emphasis upon the product as the focus of the marketing mix led Levitt to propose what he called the 'extended product concept'. According to this concept, and as shown in Figure 2.3, the product comprises three distinct elements. First, there is the *core product* which delivers the essential benefits the user is seeking and enables us to assign specific outputs to given categories — wheat, stainless steel, fractional horse power electrical motor, detergent, etc. In promoting their output, *sellers* tend to emphasise product features — size, weight, speed, colour, etc. — but *buyers* are seeking benefits which help them solve particular consumption problems. Cars, buses, railways and aeroplanes are all forms of 'transportation'; detergents are complex chemical formulations but they provide clean clothes or 'cleanliness' and, as Levitt tells us, 'purchasing agents do not buy quarter-inch drills; they buy quarter-inch holes.'

Marketers, however, deal in the *benefits* and, in so doing, they

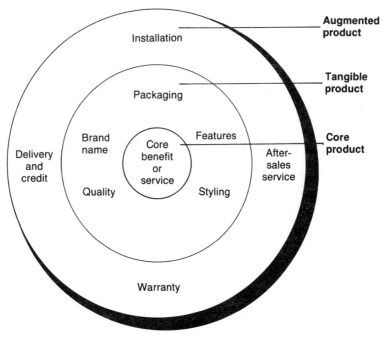

Installation — Augmented product

Packaging — Tangible product

Delivery and credit

Brand name

Core benefit or service

Features — Core product

After-sales service

Quality

Styling

Warranty

Source: Kotler (1988).

Figure 2.3 Three Levels of Product

turn core products into tangible products by investing them with specific characteristics. Kotler (1988) identifies five characteristics which he terms, 'quality level, features, styling, brand name and packaging'. Clearly, these characteristics offer the producer myriad combinations and permutations for differentiating his product from his competitors'. But, competition being what it is, competitors will quickly copy what appears to be a winning formula and so erode the innovators' advantage.

It is for this reason that in recent years producers have extended the basic product still further by 'augmenting' it with service features, such as *delivery and credit, installation, warranties* and *after-sales service*. While these may be described and even quantified, like the performance or quality of the tangible product, their real value to the consumer will depend upon his perception of them with the result that *reputation*, such as that enjoyed by IBM or

Marks & Spencer, will create a halo around the product which other competitors will find difficult to erode. (It has been estimated that it costs a firm six times as much to win a customer as to keep one. Small wonder that market leaders with large market shares do not find it difficult to defend them, provided they do not become complacent about the basis of their reputation.)

In a series of surveys undertaken by the Department of Marketing at Strathclyde University into various aspects of competitiveness, respondents were asked to rank 16 dimensions of the product in terms of contribution to their own competitive success. The results of one such survey into Queen's Award Winners for Technological Innovation and/or Export Achievement are shown in Table 2.3 below.

While the rankings provide a useful benchmark for one's own perception of the relative importance of these 16 'critical success factors' one must remember that they are the outcome of an averaging process and so do not relate to any specific firm or industry. Clearly, a design-led textile company would be more likely to rate 'design' first rather than last. The real value of the list is that it represents a distillation of the 16 most frequently cited product-related factors which sellers and buyers consider to be important to their success.

Table 2.3 Product Factors Influencing Competitiveness (in rank order)

1. Performance in operation
2. Reliability
3. Sale price
4. Efficient delivery
5. Technical sophistication
6. Quality of after-sales service
7. Durability
8. Ease of use
9. Safety in use
10. Ease of maintenance
11. Parts availability and cost
12. Attractive appearance/shape
13. Flexibility and adaptability in use
14. Advertising and promotion
15. Operator comfort
16. Design

Elsewhere (*Market Development*, 1983), Baker has argued that in making their choice, all buyers will seek to behave rationally and will base their selection upon objective performance factors related to carefully calculated cost-benefits. Of course, even this 'objectivity' is subject to mediation by the selective perception and personal preferences of the individual decision-maker but, notwithstanding this, the emergence of dominant 'brands' (industrial or consumer) is evidence that where objective superiority exists, consumers will recognise and prefer it. The paradox is that if there is a clearly superior solution then there is no choice decision! It follows that choice — the essence of competition — implies the ability to select from a group of largely indistinguishable product offerings in terms of price and performance features.

Such situations create as much dissonance and perceived risk for the industrial buyer as they do for the consumer in the supermarket faced with six brands of baked beans, frozen peas or whatever. Fortunately, the selective perception mentioned above, aided and abetted by habit, or 'learned behaviour', saves us from a breakdown. Selective perception is an in-built protective device, monitored by the subconscious, which screens out and filters the mass of information which is presented to us so that we become consciously aware of that part alone which may be relevant or important to us. Thus we are much more receptive to information about *benefits* which are important to us than we are to aspects of the product or service which are minor or inconsequential. Not only will these vary from person to person but they are likely to change over time as we learn from experience and develop new expectations. It is for this reason, as we stated earlier, that with growing choice (competition) and affluence it is unlikely that suppliers will be able to predetermine the precise benefits users are looking for without some dialogue with them. Determining the needs of users is the province of marketing research, the lack of which has been conclusively shown to be the primary cause of new product failures in the market-place. This aspect of corporate competitive behaviour is examined in the research reported in Chapter 6.

In our view, marketing research is definitely a 'non-price' competitive factor; but it is recognised as such less often than two other elements of the marketing mix — advertising and promotion — which the uninformed often regard as synonymous with the whole of marketing. Advertising and promotion have a crucial role to play in advising prospective buyers of the choice available to them and the specific benefits associated with particular product offerings. Clearly, the more information acquired by marketing research, concerning desired benefits which have been translated into product features, the easier it will be for the advertisers not only to pass on the message but also to direct this information towards those with a predisposition to receive it. How advertising works is also a subject in its own right that cannot be pursued further here. The point to be borne in mind is that, psychologically, advertising may create the 'just noticeable difference' which enables the prospective buyer to discriminate between apparently identical offerings merely by pointing out that Product X does something which is important for that buyer, while Product Y (which may also possess this attribute) neglects to do so.

The other factor to be borne in mind is that with developments in manufacturing technology and the rapid diffusion of technology, cost efficiencies from these tend to be limited and short-lived. By contrast, economies of scale in advertising, distribution and after-sales service have become significant with the result that control of the 'non-price factors' offers a greater potential for pricing flexibility than does manufacturing efficiency as the primary source of product cost.

2.5 Conclusion

In this chapter we have been chiefly concerned with establishing a framework within which to examine current issues relating to international competitiveness. To begin with, we looked at the reasons why individuals, communities and nations have found it advantageous to enter into exchange relationships. Early theories developed to show how task specialisation, added value and increased aggregate satisfaction were found wanting because of their essentially static nature. To remedy this deficiency, the technology-gap and product-life-cycle theories were developed and they offered a more satisfactory explanation of the dynamic nature of international trade. Similarly, a review of theories of

44 *Marketing and Competitive Success*

competition showed how these have changed to reflect reality. Prior to the industrial revolution, production and output were limited, and distribution and consumption were local in nature. With industrialisation, productivity increased and developments in transportation and communication resulted in significant improvements in the standard of living and a rapid population growth. These changes led to a large demand for basic goods and services which was best served by an emphasis upon product standardisation and a focus on manufacturing efficiency as the dominant managerial orientation. But as technology accelerated, population growth slowed and an endemic supply deficiency was translated into a potential for excess supply. Faced with the possibility of unsold goods, producers became more concerned with securing and holding the loyalty of consumers and so switched from a policy of product standardisation to one of product differentiation. In doing so they recognised that aggregate demand curves indicate that some consumers will pay more than others, and set out to find what additional benefits these consumers wanted for which they would pay extra. Their results highlighted the necessity to change to a market-driven strategy and emphasise product benefits rather than use price as the basis for competition. In the next chapter we will examine in more detail how changing environmental and economic conditions have resulted in distinctive managerial responses and styles.

References

Abdel-Mohsen, T.M. (1986) 'Marketing and competitiveness: a survey of current practice and performance in the UK textile machinery industry', Unpublished Ph.D., University of Strathclyde.
Baker, M.J. (1983) *Market Development: A Comprehensive Study*, Penguin Books.
Baker, M.J. (1985) *Marketing: An Introductory Text*, 4th edn, Macmillan.
Chamberlin, E. (1933) *Theory of Monopolistic Competition*, Cambridge University Press.
Freeman, C. (1963) 'The plastics industry: a comparative study of research and innovation', *National Institute Economic Review*, vol. 16, November.
Hirsch, S. (1967) *Location of Industry and International Competitiveness*, Clarendon Press.
Kotler, P. (1988) *Marketing Management: Analysis, Planning, Implementation and Control*, 6th edn, Prentice-Hall.

Leontief, W. (1954) 'Domestic production and foreign trade: the American capital position re-examined', *Economic International*, vol. II, no. 1, February.
Levitt, T. (1977) 'Marketing when things change', *Harvard Business Review*, November–December.
Ohlin, B. (1933) *Interregional and International Trade*, Harvard University Press.
Posner, M.V. (1961) 'International trade and technical change', *Oxford Economic Papers*, vol. xxxi.
Ricardo, David (1817) *The Principles of Political Economy and Taxation*, Cambridge University Press.
Rogers, Everett M. (1962) *Diffusion of Innovations*, The Free Press.
Rothwell, R. (1981) 'Non-price factors in the export competitiveness of agricultural engineering products', *Science Policy Research*, vol. 10.
Rothwell, R. (1983) 'Design matters more than price', *Design*, January.
Simon, H.A. and March, J.G. (1959) *Organisations*, John Wiley.
Sloan, A. (1963) *My Years at General Motors*, Doubleday.
Smith, Adam (1776) *The Wealth of Nations*, Modern Library edn.
Vernon, R.G. (1966) 'International investment and international trade in the product cycle', *Quarterly Journal of Economics*, vol. 80, no. 2, May.
Walker, W.B. (1979) *Industrial Innovation and International Trading Performance*, J.A.I. Press Inc., Greenwich, Ct.
Wells, L.T. Jr (1984) 'International trade: the product life cycle approach', in R. Mayer (ed.) *International Business*, Wiley.

3

Change, Competition and Marketing

3.1 Change, Competition and Marketing

In the preceding chapter we examined a variety of explanations for the benefits which will accrue if the concept of task specialisation is extended from the small self-sufficient community, in which it first developed, to exchanges between national economies. From this review it became apparent that early theories of absolute and comparative advantage were an inadequate explanation of the real world as we know it today, just as the economic theories of pure and perfect competition and of monopoly may have described the situation in the eighteenth century but, nowadays, define the boundaries within which real competition occurs. That this should be so is unsurprising. Early theorists developed explanations of exchange and competition from their observation of the world in which they lived. Over time the world has moved on as individuals, firms and economies have striven to improve their standard of living. The material benefits of technological innovation and industrialisation have resulted in massive social and political change and have necessitated a radical reappraisal of the forces of supply and demand, production, and consumption. Thus, more recent theories of competition and international trade have sought to take on board the observed reality and to develop explanations (theories) which will help us anticipate and even predict future behaviour. In the process, and given the experiences of the past two decades, there has developed an attitude of mind which questions whether this is possible. 'Accelerating change', 'turbulence', 'knowledge-based society' and many similar phrases are bandied about to justify

46

the view that we are on the threshold of an entirely novel experience ('Brave New World'?) which we are well equipped to deal with.

3.2 Plus Ça Change . . .

It is an intrinsic element of human nature that we all like to think we are somehow different from our fellow men. Thus, as generation succeeds generation, we are exhorted to look to the future and not to live in the past. In so doing there is a tendency to overlook and neglect the lessons which we might learn from the past that would significantly improve our performance today. But, while today's managers are firmly convinced of the relevance and application of the experience curve concept, they largely ignore the aphorism that while wise men learn from other men's experience, fools find out for themselves.

Of course the world is changing, and we must adapt to these changes if we are to survive. However, in the same sense that one cannot step in the same river twice, we should be willing to accept that while the river may have changed in degree, the problem of crossing it is conceptually the same — it is only the possible solutions which may have changed. The thrust of this chapter is that although the problems facing the present generation of senior management are significantly different in both degree and kind from those which faced their immediate predecessors, they are not novel in themselves.

The view that there is nothing fundamentally new about the economic and managerial problems which currently face us is based upon the observation that change is essentially an evolutionary *not* revolutionary process. Evidence in support of this belief is implicit in the concept of the business 'cycle'. This idea is reviewed briefly as a prelude to a discussion of the changes which have occurred in the second half of this century and which are cited in support of the proposition that things are different today. Specifically, it is argued that the nature of competition has changed and that if the British economy is to halt an apparently irreversible decline then it must undertake a radical reappraisal of its policies and practices. The basis and validity of these arguments are examined and lead naturally to a discussion of the nature of competitiveness and the factors underlying success or failure in the market-place.

As we saw in the previous chapter, analysis of key success factors points unequivocally to the fact that while cost and price elements are still of vital importance, it is usually non-price factors which determine success in the market-place. Collectively, many non-price factors have been subsumed within the areas of marketing and design and the chapter closed by looking at the evidence from a recent survey which points convincingly to the conclusion that these two activities are strongly associated with superior competitive performance. That said, it is obviously as true today as it always has been that making a better product at the same or lower price than your competitors is the only certain guarantee of success.

3.3   Cycles and Waves

As we established in Chapter 1, since the middle of this century there have been radical changes in both the composition and balance of trade between nations. The effects of these changes upon the UK economy have been deep and wide-ranging and have led to the virtual extinction of industries once central to our industrial power, like shipbuilding and motor cycles, and the decimation of others such as steel and textiles. Increased import penetration and declining shares of export markets formerly dominated by British goods underline the acute concern for our declining competitiveness as a trading nation. But in this we are not alone, and the extent and magnitude of the oscillations between recession and growth have prompted many analysts and commentators to characterise the era as 'turbulent'.

There is a considerable body of evidence to suggest that 'turbulence' is a phenomenon which occurs in a wide variety of contexts when the continuation of established trends is threatened. The evidence also indicates that these trends, such as economic growth and the technological innovation which underlies it, proceed in a cyclical manner, — hence the 'economic', 'trade' or 'business cycle' and the 'product life cycle'. Economic forecasters and marketing planners, respectively, have attempted to use these perceived regularities for purposes of forecasting and prediction, but usually with very mixed and limited success. In our view these attempts — which usually result in rejection of the 'model' on the grounds that it does not work — are misguided. The *idea* of a business or product cycle is just that — it provides a framework for reflecting upon a phenomenon and devising strategies for its manipulation and control. Implementing these strategies in the particular is likely to require highly specific solutions which differ so widely as to defy the generalisation implicit in the concept.

If we appear to stray, it is with a purpose. Given that analysis confirms the existence of business cycles, then it follows that analysis of previous cycles should equip us better to cope with present conditions. Figure 3.1 represents a stylised representation of the economic cycle, and Figure 3.2 the biological life cycle (from which product-life-cycle theory is derived). Clearly, both are very similar, and both propose an evolutionary process in which periods of rapid growth/development result in instability which may result in one of three basic outcomes:

- Success — growth continues
- Stabilisation
- Failure — decline sets in

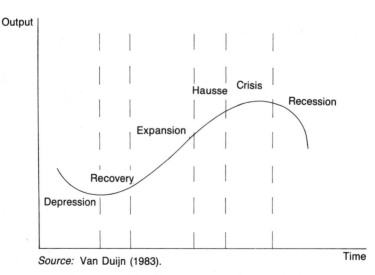

Source: Van Duijn (1983).

Figure 3.1 The Phases of an Economic Cycle

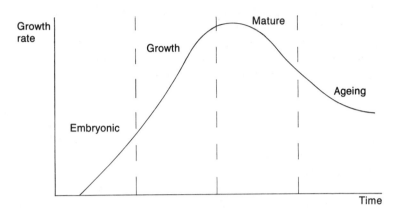

Figure 3.2 The Biological Life Cycle

In the case of both cycles it is important to distinguish clearly the level of aggregation at which we are operating. Thus the fact that biological organisms continue to evolve and grow, as does the world economy, does not mean that specific species, economies, industries or products may not stabilise, decline or become extinct. The point we are seeking to make is that while one generation of managers may have 'grown up' under conditions of continuous growth and so be ill-equipped *by experience* to cope with turbulence, this does not mean they cannot learn from the distilled wisdom (knowledge and theory) of previous generations of managers who have survived such conditions successfully.

It is surely not without significance that many of the world's largest and most influential corporations were the survivors of earlier periods of upheaval and turbulence. Certainly, most would agree that the recessions of the 1890s (and the antitrust legislation at the same period), the 1920s and the 1930s were probably more severe than that which we faced in the 1970s. Despite this Standard Oil, United States Steel, ICI, General Motors, Unilever and many others emerged triumphant. It would be surprising if we could learn nothing from their example.

Certainly, to suggest that a new breed of managers with no experience at all could cope better would seem extravagant. After all, if progress is evolutionary, the survivors are those who can *adapt*, as can be seen in the case of those firms which have survived the recent shake-up in British industry. It also lends considerable force to the view that if you really want to discover the secrets of successful management you should analyse the performance and techniques of managers who are successful in declining or 'sunset' industries. After all, if demand is expanding rapidly, managerial mistakes are less critical to success, and it is only when maturity sets in that the need for professional management skills becomes apparent — as with Sinclair and Apple in the market for personal computers.

If, therefore, we are to address successfully a concern for the declining competitiveness of British industry it would seem sensible to base the prognosis upon careful diagnosis. In turn, careful analysis requires, first, that we identify the causes of the current turbulence which have led to this decline and, second, that we seek to compare this diagnosis with precedent to see if the latter can provide guidelines for future action.

3.4 The Frantic Fifties

Although detailed analysis reveals fluctuations in the fortunes of the economies of the industrialised world during the 1950s, the overwhelming impression is one of postwar reconstruction and burgeoning growth. However, once the pent-up demand for consumer goods — which had been frustrated by the war years — was satiated, the incipient causes of the prewar Depression began to make themselves felt again. Whether these causes are seen as arising from excess supply or scarce demand the result is much the same — too many goods chasing too few people and a marked increase in competition. (Does this ring a bell?)

It is hardly surprising that increased competition first becomes apparent in the market for fast-moving consumer goods for, while these are essential to life, there is a finite limit to the amounts of food and drink which one can consume. This fact is enshrined in Engels' Law which states that as an individual's income increases, the proportion spent on food declines. Faced with a near-saturated market and intense competition, it is unsurprising that suppliers should seek ways to protect their own positions and that to do so they should try to distinguish or differentiate themselves from their immediate competitors as the first step to building preference for, then loyalty to, their offering.

Traditionally, economists' models of competition have centred upon price as the mechanism by which supply and demand are brought into equilibrium in the market-place. According to the model, if supply exceeds demand then the price will fall until it is sufficiently low to attract new demand into the market thus absorbing the excess supply. Conversely, if demand exceeds supply then the price will be increased as a 'rationing' device until, once again, the quantity demanded precisely balances the available supply. However, as we have seen, 'perfect competition' and the 'perfect' market are essentially figments of the theoretician's imagination, designed to define one end of a spectrum of competitive states which range from the pure or perfect state, where price and the market determine the equilibrium between supply and demand, to the opposite extreme of monopoly, where a single producer exercises complete control over supply and so can dictate price and the volume of demand he will satisfy.

While the models are far more complex and sophisticated than implied by this simplistic description, this is largely irrelevant to the fact that there are very few (if any) examples of either perfect competition or monopoly. In reality, competition is largely imperfect. Monopoly, by definition, cannot really be a *competitive* state for competition requires more than one protagonist. Similarly, the basic assumptions of perfect competition — such as perfect information and a totally homogeneous product — are rarely, if ever, satisfied.

It follows that competition is imperfect to a greater or lesser degree, depending upon how far the reality departs from the assumptions. However, it was not until the 1930s that the economists Robinson and Chamberlin independently articulated a theory of imperfect competition which reflected the reality of a market-place in which suppliers pursued a strategy of product differentiation in an attempt to establish a temporary monopoly over a segment of the total market. Clearly, if you can position your product or service in the consumer's mind as different from other close substitutes then you can escape the straightjacket of the market price and exercise at least some control over price. As we shall see later, it matters little whether the differentiating factor is objective or subjective so long as it is perceived as such by the potential user and is considered important by him.

The importance of this further reprise of economic theory is contained entirely in the last sentence, in which it is recognised that the ultimate determinant of success or failure is the consumer's perception of a product or service. Thus, it was in the 1950s that the search for competitive advantage persuaded producers of the need to define precisely the needs of their prospective customers and thereby led to the rediscovery of what is now universally recognised as 'the marketing concept'. In simpler and less sophisticated times producer and user were usually in direct contact with one another, and the possibility of distortion or misunderstanding of the user's need was minimal. Given the separation of producer and user, which has accompanied task specialisation and industrialisation, together with the concentration of production that has resulted from the pursuit of scale economies, it is small wonder that producers were in increasing danger of losing contact with the specific needs of their customers. Under the circumstances it would seem obvious that suppliers should take direct action to determine the precise nature of demand and modify their supply accordingly.

It cannot be over-emphasised that attempting to determine customer needs *prior* to production (a strategy of market segmentation) is quite different from seeking to modify one's existing output in an effort (trial and error selling) to establish more precisely the nature of demand. The latter tactic of product differentiation is symptomatic of a 'sell what we can make' or production orientation; the former is due to a 'make what we can sell' or marketing orientation. However, while some accepted the logic of the marketing concept, many did not with the result that the 1960s may be regarded as the decade of ...

3.5 The Consumer Revolt

Although 'materialism' has always attracted its critics, their views fell largely upon the deaf ears of a population which was denied the excesses described. But the increased affluence of the population of the advanced economies, and the methods and practices adopted by manufacturers to exploit this opportunity, changed all this.

Amongst the first populist writers to attract wide attention was Vance Packard, whose *Hidden Persuaders* (1957) promoted an

Orwellian view that big business was brainwashing consumers into purchasing products they did not really want. This was a major indictment of advertising and selling which, of necessity, assume a much larger role in determining consumer preference when one is faced with a wide selection of competing products with identical performance characteristics and prices. The 'big business is bad for you' theme was also promoted in Packard's *The Waste Makers* (1960) in which he attacked some of the excesses and consequences of a materialistic society. Packard's indictment was picked up with enthusiasm by Ralph Nader, whose *Unsafe At Any Speed* (1966) was a chilling picture of uncaring car manufacturers who cut corners in product design and manufacture in order to swell the corporate coffers and had scant regard for the lives of their customers. General Motors attempted to discredit Nader but only succeeded in losing a highly publicised court case from which Nader emerged as the hero of the consumer revolt.

More general criticism — such as Rachel Carson's *Silent Spring* (1962) in which she described a world devoid of wildlife as a consequence of chemical farming — initiated a green movement which enjoys political representation in many governments and led, in 1986, to some rather frosty exchanges between the Prime Ministers of Norway and the UK. Concurrently, thinking businessmen began to pay heed to the groundswell of anti-materialistic sentiment, and initiated their own inquiries into the implications of the consumerists' clarion call for fewer, but better, products offering greater value for money, but with a less profligate use of scarce resources. The Club of Rome's *The Limits to Growth* (1972) may well have been the catalyst for a response to the latter requirement in the early 1970s but an answer to the 'value for money' lobby was already on its way and from an unexpected source.

3.6 The Rise of the Phoenix

So much has been written about the West German and Japanese economies that only passing reference need be made here to the phenomenon of two economies devastated by war and emerging from the ashes as leading trading nations in the world.

Many would argue that almost total destruction of an economy creates a golden opportunity to reconstruct it, but very few would possess the resolve to do so. Thus, while academics frequently offer the advice that it would make sense to start again with a clean sheet rather than attempt to patch up an ailing concern, not many practitioners take up the suggestion, even though the Japanese and German examples point to the long-term benefits of radical, as opposed to gradualist, solutions. However, our exemplars had no choice — it was either sink or swim — and the lesson to be learned is from what they did rather than why they did it. In very simplified terms the Phoenix strategy would seem to comprise the following steps:

1. Acquire the best available technology (it has been estimated that for an outlay of $3 billion in the 1950s, Japan secured the rights to all the Western world's R & D and has used this as the foundation for its own investment).
2. Secure the home base — concentrate first upon the needs of the domestic market and set out to make what you can sell, i.e. adopt a marketing orientation.
3. Offer the highest possible quality consistent with the asking price.
4. Accept that responsibility does not end when the product leaves the factory gate — ensure adequate channels of distribution and provide appropriate after-sales service.
5. Concentrate resources and do not over-reach yourself — i.e. do not seek to enter a new market until you have developed the necessary infrastructure and support systems, and have secured a dominant or leadership position in the markets you are in.
6. Be patient — seek to build long-term, lasting relationships rather than make a quick profit.
7. Research your markets continuously and modify your offering to match changing needs, i.e. consolidate your position.

Taken together these steps represent an almost irresistible strategy founded on the basic rule for business success — build a better product than your competitors at an equivalent or lower price, and make it readily available to consumers. If you follow this precept, then whether you make steel, machine tools, textile machinery, consumer electronics or whatever, you will succeed

— a fact learned painfully in the UK, as leading firms and even whole industries, like motor-cycle manufacturing, were displaced from the market.

But worse was to come — while the First World debated the implications of *Limits to Growth*, the Third World acted upon it and began to ration basic raw materials, particularly oil, and so attacked the very foundations of Western materialism. This, more than anything else, initiated the instability, if not crisis, of the 1970s (discussed earlier in the context of evolutionary cycles) and raises the question addressed here: 'How do we break through the barriers to economic growth arising from our declining competitiveness in world markets?'

3.7 Back from the Brink

The first step in the treatment of any problem must be awareness that it exists and, second, that it is of sufficient consequence to merit careful analysis. While the first condition — declining competitiveness — has been apparent for several decades now, it was only in the 1970s that the symptoms became sufficiently acute for them to be taken seriously. Like ageing or a wasting disease, initially one can compensate or adjust for loss of a capacity but, eventually, one is reduced to vital functions — the loss of which can only have one outcome.

Fundamentally, the basic economic problem of maximising satisfaction from the consumption of scarce resources resolves itself into a question of the appropriate unit of analysis. The ideal, theoretical solution would be to treat the whole world as a single economy and pursue the theory of comparative advantage to its logical conclusion, through universal free trade. Nationalism, politics, culture, stages of economic development, barriers to trade, etc. make this both impractical and unrealistic. On the other hand, enlightened self-interest rejects the other extreme of self-sufficiency and protectionism, and the compromise is a mixture of both free-trade and protectionist policies with the emphasis depending upon the economies' basic resource endowment. Thus the UK and Japan, with a limited base, opt for trade, while the USA is more self-sufficient and protectionist in its policies.

It is true that Britain's share of world trade has been declining since the middle of the last century — at which time we accounted for almost 50 per cent and so, by definition, could not increase our share — but the decline was comparatively slow and over-whelmed, in volume terms, by the absolute growth in world trade. But, consider what has happened since 1950 — as Kerry Schott (1984) has pointed out, we then enjoyed a 25 per cent market share of the world trade in manufactures, but by 1986 this had declined to only 6 per cent. Perhaps the only consolation to be drawn from Figure 1.2 (Chapter 1), which records this, is that for the last 10 years we have begun to hold our position better. Schott points out: 'This loss in market share of world manufac-turing appears to have largely gone to West Germany and Japan. During the 1950–81 period, West Germany increased its market share of these world exports from 7 per cent to 18 per cent; and over the same period Japan increased its share from just 3 per cent in 1950 to 18 per cent in 1981'. She concludes that UK in-dustry has lost its ability to compete in export markets for manufactured goods — a view strongly supported by the analysis in Chapter 1.

While declining export competitiveness is not good news, it would be of less consequence if the UK balance of trade was kept in equilibrium by a reduction in imports. Unfortunately, as Figure 1.7 (Chapter 1) shows, the problem has been compounded by an increase in import penetration that has grown as rapidly as our export performance has declined. The consequence is a trade deficit for many products where previously we enjoyed a signifi-cant competitive advantage.

Clearly, this situation has not developed overnight and there has been no shortage of investigation and reports identifying the problem, analysing its causes and prescribing courses of action to alleviate, if not reverse, the trends. So what's different now to suggest we may have backed off from the brink of economic disaster? At least two things: first, the Americans have contracted the 'British disease'; second, the UK has had, since 1979, a government dedicated to restoring competitiveness.

American complacency — which to some extent must be con-doned, by virtue of the fact that it is the world's richest economy — was finally broken by the publication of an article entitled 'Managing our way to economic decline' by Bob Hayes and Bill Abernathy which appeared in the July/August 1980 issue of the

Harvard Business Review. In drawing attention to the USA's declining competitiveness in international markets and the import penetration of domestic markets, such as automobiles and electronics, which it had 'invented', Hayes and Abernathy pointed out that even the UK had outperformed the USA in terms of economic growth over the past two decades! The diagnosis? — an overemphasis upon a financial/sales orientation, the key features of which may be summarised as:

- The emphasis tends to be upon short-range profit at the expense of growth and longer-range profit.
- Budgeting and forecasting frequently pre-empt business planning.
- Efficiency may outrank effectiveness as a management criterion.
- Pricing, cost, credit, service and other policies may be based on false economy influences and lack of market-place realism.
- The business focus is not on the customer and market but on internal considerations and numbers.

The impact of this pungent criticism (and others like it) stimulated an upsurge of interest in possible remedies to cure the problem. One manifestation of this has been the enormous upsurge of interest in management books, putting several of them like *In Search of Excellence, One Minute Manager, Megatrends* and *Iacocca* into the all-time best-seller lists. Significantly, these books possess a number of common features:

- They assert the superiority of American management and systems (particularly over the Japanese about whom Kenneth Blanchard — author of *One Minute Manager* — jokes: 'I often say that the second biggest mistake that the Japanese made after Pearl Harbor was to keep beating hell out of us about productivity').
- They stress entrepreneurial values and the money-making ethic so strongly challenged by the consumerist movement of the 1960s and 1970s.
- They are based upon the analysis of the practice and procedure of firms or people who are leaders in their field and manifestly successful.

- They reduce the ingredients of success to simple catechisms or formulae.
- They emphasise that the essential catalyst and hero of the piece is the manager himself.

American ideas on business and management have long been influential on this side of the Atlantic. But, for the last 30 years, it has been generally conceded that stop—go government policies and an industrial relations climate dominated by the trade unions have not exactly been conducive to effective management. As a leader in the *Sunday Times* observed:

> Perhaps it is wrong to be too hard on Britain's managers. After all, they are not used to power. For decades they reeled before the unions. They conceded control of their shopfloors to shop stewards and they shied away from innovating or investing in new technology because the unions might not like it, or might demand so much Danegeld for allowing change to happen that change became an unpleasant, troublesome concept for managers. These inhibitions no longer exist, by and large, in most British companies, in the seventh year of the Thatcher revolution. But management, especially when it comes to pay demands, still behave as if they do. After so many years of union dominance it looks as if Britain's managers have forgotten how to manage. (21/9/1986)

To have forgotten implies we once knew how — a point made earlier about not re-inventing the wheel, and reinforced by the review of our past trading performance. It is only because we were once so successful that anyone bothers to comment now that we are less so. What then was the basis for our success and how can we regain our lost glory?

3.8 A Crisis of Confidence

In 1987 the *Financial Times* ran a short series on 'the guru factor', which examined the recent popularity of business books of the kind discussed above. Implicit in the common features cited was the need to overcome insecurity engendered by the social intro-spection following Vietnam and 'le défi japonais' and to restore confidence in the money-making ethic which had sustained American entrepreneurs and managers in the past. Much the

same is required in the UK but on a much grander scale, a point
stressed in the *Sunday Times* leader quoted earlier:

> For much of this century business has not been fashionable in this
> country. The upper classes have considered it vulgar, the middle
> classes have preferred the respectability of the professions and the
> working classes have seen themselves locked in conflict with it. The
> combination of these attitudes has contributed to our industrial decline
> by impoverishing our business class over the years so that today it
> lacks the confidence, ability or status of its counterparts in America,
> Japan or West Germany.

Changing these attitudes cannot be accomplished overnight
(assuming that society at large is sufficiently aware of the implications of *not* doing so to be prepared to make the effort). While
it may be a long-term objective, it is important to remember that
although an attitude may be a 'predisposition to behave in a given
way' there is ample evidence that attitudinal change may both
precede or follow behavioural change. Under the circumstances,
it would seem sensible to try and enhance behavioural change,
if for no other reason than that if you have persevered with the
argument this far then it is reasonable to assume you already
possess a favourable attitude to business but would like to
improve performance.

While we admit that retelling our business history and
emphasising past deeds of entrepreneurial derring-do may help
restore some confidence and strengthen our resolve, it is not
enough to help cope with the conditions facing UK industry
today. The analysis of changes in competition since 1950 indicates
beyond doubt that the conditions which prevail today are
significantly different from those of the past. In a nutshell, we
now have the technological capacity not only to create excess supplies of any industrial or consumer good you care to name but,
beyond that, we also have the ability to customise these goods
to meet the specific needs of individuals. So what advice can
academicians offer practitioners?

3.9   Never Mind the Width, Look at the Quality

In promoting the cause of marketing, many evangelists felt it
necessary to discredit the idolatry of the past and criticise the

deficiencies of the 'production orientation' which the new religion would sweep away. Such criticisms were naive, immature and misguided. Faced with an endemic supply deficiency, past generations of managers were entirely correct to pursue a policy of 'the mostest for the leastest'. What is more, under such circumstances of scarcity, need and priorities are largely self-evident and you do not need an extensive market intelligence system to tell you what is already apparent.

As we have observed earlier, the golden rule for business success is 'build a better product for the same or lower price than your competitors'. This rule is as true today as it has always been. What is different is that technology changes and diffuses so rapidly now that it is becoming increasingly difficult to sustain an *objective* product difference and sellers must turn increasingly to non-objective or subjective factors with an emphasis upon quality and value for money. This is not to say one can ignore product and cost/price factors — indeed product performance factors like 'reliability' invariably top surveys of customer satisfaction, and while 'price' may not assume the priority status accorded it in economic theory it still figures as an important criterion in consumer choice. However, in determining the performance factors which should be improved and promoted to prospective customers one can depend far less upon one's intuitive feel for the market than in the past. It is here that the marketing function has a contribution to make, particularly in adding value through the identification and development of non-price factors.

Adoption of a marketing orientation requires an organisation to recognise the customer and his satisfaction as its raison d'être and to organise all its activities towards the achievement of this goal. It follows that the first step in developing a marketing orientation must be a comprehensive understanding of the needs and behaviour of one's existing and prospective customers.

3.10 Conclusion

The basic arguments deployed in this chapter have been as follows:

1. The current turbulence in the economic and competitive environment is not, in and of itself, a new experience. It

follows that, in addressing the problems it presents, we should take due account of past experience.

2. That said, the specific factors leading to the current problems are different in degree and, if nothing else, reflect technological change and a shift in the balance of competitive power between the advanced economies.

3. Diagnosis of the nature of competitive advantage indicates that it is based upon a better understanding of consumer needs (a marketing orientation) and its translation into products and services which offer better quality and value for money.

While limited in scope it is hoped that the analysis, diagnosis and prognosis carry conviction. What is crystal clear from all the evidence is that, ultimately, it is the knowledge (theory), skill (experience) and commitment of management which distinguish between success and failure in today's competitive market-place.

In the next chapter we examine in some detail the findings of other researchers and writers who have examined managerial practice and performance in an attempt to distill the absolute essence of the nature of competitive success.

References

Baker, M.J., Hart S., Black, C. and Abdel-Mohsen, T.M. (1986) 'The contribution of marketing to competitive success: a literature review', *Journal of Marketing Management*, vol. 2, no. 1, Summer, pp. 39–61.
Black, C. and Baker, M.J. (1986) *Profit by Design*, A Report prepared for the Design Council — Scotland and Scottish Development Agency, Department of Marketing, University of Strathclyde, July.
Carson, R. (1962) *Silent Spring*, Houghton Mifflin Co.
Chamberlin, E. (1933) *Theory of Monopolistic Competition*, Cambridge University Press.
Club of Rome (1972) *The Limits to Growth*.
Hayes, R. and Abernathy, W. (1980) 'Managing our way to economic decline', *Harvard Business Review*, July/August.
Nader, R. (1966) *Unsafe At Any Speed*, Pocket Books.
Packard, V. (1957) *The Hidden Persuaders*, David McKay Co.
Packard, V. (1960) *The Waste Makers*, David McKay Co.
Robinson, Joan (1933) *The Economics of Imperfect Competition*, Macmillan.
Roy, R. and Bruce, M. (1984) *Product Design, Innovation and Competition*

in British Manufacturing: Background, Aims and Methods, Working Paper WP-02, Design Innovation Group, The Open University, September.

Schott, K. (1984), 'Economic competitiveness and design', *The Royal Society of Arts Journal,* vol. CXXXII, no. 5338, September, pp. 648–655.

Van Duijn, J.A. (1983) *The Long Wave in Economic Life,* Allen and Unwin.

Wilkins, A.L. and Ouchi, W.G. (1983) 'Efficient cultures: exploring the relationship between culture and organisational performance', *Administrative Science Quarterly,* vol. 28.

4

Critical Success Factors

4.1 Introduction

In the previous chapter, it emerged that the adoption of a marketing orientation is necessary in order to achieve customer satisfaction and thus business success. Conceptually, such an orientation stresses the sovereignty of the customers, placing them at the beginning of the exchange process, not at its end. There is now a considerable body of knowledge, which is based on empirical evidence, of the importance of marketing at many levels of business activity. This said, it would be wrong to suggest that no other factors might influence the commercial performance of a firm.

The purpose of this chapter is twofold. First, it overviews the factors which are known to influence the competitive performance of a company. Second, it explores in greater detail the scope and nature of one of those factors — marketing.

4.2 Factors Influencing Success

Management writers and researchers seeking to explain the influences on competitiveness have tended to emphasise five 'sets' of factors: environmental, organisational, strategic, managerial, and marketing. These are shown in Figure 4.1, and the first four are briefly described below.

Environmental Factors

The first set of factors which can be used to explain an organisation's performance relates to the environment where the organisa-

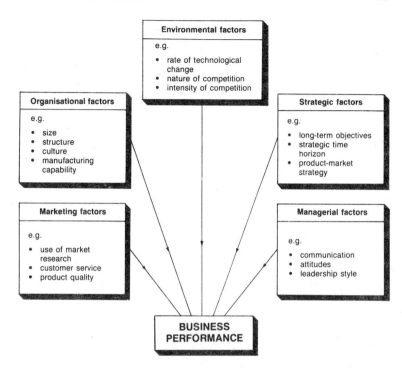

Figure 4.1 Factors Influencing Competitive Success

tion is operating. Factors in the environment, such as the rate of technological change, have been seen to act as a deterministic influence to which organisations adapt their structures and processes, in order to survive and grow. By way of illustration: one of the most successful sectors of British manufacturing industry — electronic components — is characterised by rapid technological change and demand which is increasing at a rate not matched by the amount of product that manufacturers can actually supply (ICC *Business Performance Analysis* 1986–8).

It is clear that a company's performance is likely to be improved in mass, growing and uncompetitive markets. Indeed much of the work in this area has suggested that the rate of technological change and the intensity of market competition are the most important environmental properties affecting an organisation's functioning and performance (Neghandi and Reimann 1973,

Khandwalla 1977 and Emery and Trist 1965). In a similar way, Cooper (1979) identified eleven factors affecting the success of new product introductions, three of which relate to techno-economic factors. He concluded that avoiding dynamic markets with many new product introductions, avoiding competitive markets, and focusing on a high-need growth market were among those factors which differentiated new product success from failure.

Organisational Factors

Management writers have detailed the way in which organisational variables modify company performance. A first example of organisational factors is the *structure* of the organisation. As mentioned above, organisational structure is often an attempt to cope with the demands of the environment. Thus, according to Burns and Stalker (1961), firms operating in fast-changing environments are best served by an 'organic', or a loose and flexible, structure. Conversely, firms operating in stable environments will function best with a 'mechanistic', or tightly-controlled, organisational structure. Almost twenty years later, the work of Peters and Waterman (1982), Kanter (1983) and Peters and Austin (1986) reaffirms this contention. They found that the excellent companies in their sample tended to adopt a 'simple form' with 'lean staff'. A very recent British replication of *In Search of Excellence* (Saunders and Wong 1985) found that in businesses with a divisional structure, where autonomy and entrepreneurship are encouraged, performance was enhanced.

A second example of organisational factors is the *culture* of the organisation. Corporate culture refers to the system of shared values within an organisation, which is increasingly seen to be of importance in explaining the relative success of business enterprises. Wilkins and Ouchi (1983) explore the relationship between organisational culture and performance, concluding that culture affects both efficiency and profit.

To support this contention further, Dunn, Norburn and Birley (1985) draw on empirical evidence to suggest a positive association between corporate culture and company performance.

Specifically, companies which performed well tended to share the following values and beliefs:

(i) a belief in being best;
(ii) a belief in the importance of the individual;
(iii) a belief in superior quality and service;
(iv) a belief in innovation;
(v) a belief in informal communication.

In general, it is becoming increasingly accepted that even the best thought-out strategy will not achieve expectations if it does not fit in with the 'social norms' of the company (Gagliardi 1986 and Muhlbacher, Vyslozil and Ritter 1987).

A third example of organisational factors is the *manufacturing capability* of the firm, sometimes expressed as 'operations technology' (Khandwalla 1977). More recently, Abernathy, Clark and Kantrow (1981) identified superior manufacturing processes as a source of competitive advantage among Japanese and some European companies — in industries such as machine tools, minicomputers, commercial aircraft and textile machinery. Similarly, Hayes and Wheelwright (1984) lament the relative neglect of attention to manufacturing as a potent force in achieving competitive success, while Hill's (1985) book, *Manufacturing Strategy*, underlines the importance of manufacturing in the achievement of corporate goals.

Strategic Factors

There is a good deal of evidence to suggest that strategic factors are essential to the survival and growth of companies. Strategic factors include the strategic planning process and content of strategic plans. The work of Thune and House (1970) concluded that companies that relied on formal strategic planning performed better than companies that did not. Similarly, a recent review of the value of strategic planning by Brownlie (1985a and b) cites the studies of Karger and Malik (1975), Ansoff (1968), and Schoeffler, Buzzell and Heany (1974) in support of the view that strategic planning enhances company performance.

The content of strategic plans and the nature of strategic objectives have also been shown to affect competitive success. Hooley and Lynch (1985) found that the so-called 'High-Fliers' — that is, companies performing well — were significantly different from the 'Also-Rans' in terms of the extent of formal long-range planning they carried out, and the content of plans and the approach to planning. The National Economic Development Office (NEDO 1979) lends support to the proposition that the nature of a firm's goals fundamentally affects its ability and willingness to change. The on-going work of Doyle, Saunders and Wong (1985) showed, for example, that a company can improve profitability by either raising volume or improving productivity (see Figure 4.2). Thus, the strategic focus for raising volume is twofold: compete or innovate. Either route is seen as an offensive stance. On the other hand, the strategic focus for improving productivity involves reducing costs, rationalising the product mix, or increasing prices. This so-called British solution is basically defensive, as demonstrated by the study which compared the strategic focus of British and Japanese companies: the Japanese favoured the aggressive focus.

Saunders and Wong (1985) not only found that the content of strategic plans differed between successful and less successful companies, but that the time horizon of planning differed between the two, with successful firms more committed to both medium- and long-range plans.

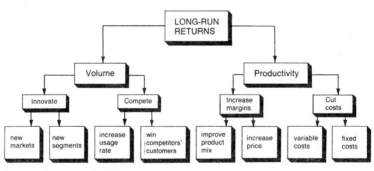

Source: Saunders (1987).

Figure 4.2

Managerial Factors

The first element in 'managerial factors' is *managerial communication*. In the excellent companies described by Peters and Waterman (1982), communication tended to be informal and intense, often encouraged by physical supports such as blackboards. Kanter's work confirms this view. In their replication of *In Search of Excellence*, Saunders and Wong (1985) found that informal communication distinguished the successful from the less successful in their sample of 30 companies. In a CBI study (Matthews 1985), it was reported that rapidly growing companies appear to attach great importance to encouraging the widest possible dissemination of information throughout the company.

A second element of managerial factors is *style*. Eastlack and MacDonald's (1970) study described eight managerial styles which affect both the sales growth and return on investment of enterprises. Chief Executive Officers whose companies most often recorded both high sales growth and above-average profit performance were 'growth entrepreneurs' and 'R & D planners'. Growth entrepreneurs were found in small companies, aiming for very rapid sales increases. They were also very active in all areas fostering growth: formulating goals and implementing plans, for example. On the other hand, R & D planners were found in medium-to-large corporations which invested heavily in new product development. These CEOs were involved in the strategic selection of new product areas and viewed their companies as pioneers or market leaders.

The McKinsey study (1983) of American growth companies found that the style of CEOs shared three common traits: (i) persevering to the point of obsession; (ii) builders, not bankers; and (iii) calculated risk takers. Ames (1970) and Webster (1981) complain of the often unimaginative style of corporate leaders. Webster associates this lack of imagination with the humdrum performance of many companies.

These questions of managerial style and leadership are becoming more and more prevalent in discussions of what contributes to competitive success (Marlow 1984; Oakley 1984, 1985; Bennis and Nanus 1985; Goldsmith and Clutterbuck 1984; Vaill 1982; and Saunders 1987). Examination of the fifth set of factors — marketing — is central to the rest of the chapter.

4.3   The Contribution of Marketing

From its very beginnings, marketing has been ill-defined and misunderstood, so a definition of terms is essential at this juncture. In the *Macmillan Dictionary of Marketing and Advertising* (1984) a number of authors are quoted to reflect the diversity of definitions of marketing. A number of the recurrent ideas contained in these definitions are essentially that marketing is: determining and satisfying consumer demands; performing business activities that direct the flow of goods and services from producer to consumer or user; buying, selling, transporting and storing goods; delivering a standard of living; the whole business, seen from the customer's point of view. There appears to be a general consensus in definitions, but no single definition. An explanation for this is put forward:

> Marketing, however, has no recognised central theoretical basis such as exists for many other disciplines, notably the physical sciences, and, in some cases, the behavioural sciences. (Halbert 1965)

For a more complete review of marketing definitions, the reader is referred to Crosier's (1975) article, 'What exactly is marketing?'

It is virtually impossible to discuss the nature of marketing without reference to the ubiquitous *marketing concept*. Its simple and intuitive appeal comes from its focus on the customer as the motivating force behind an exchange. However, definitions of the marketing concept are as prolific as definitions of marketing. Again, the *Macmillan Dictionary of Marketing and Advertising* proves a helpful source of information.

> Essentially, it [the marketing concept] would seem to consist of three basic elements:
> (a) a consumer orientation by which is meant the belief that the consumer should be the centre of all the organisation's thinking and activity;
> (b) an orientation which seeks to coordinate and integrate all the organisation's efforts towards common goals;
> (c) a profit orientation by which the company seeks to achieve its goals through maximising consumer satisfaction rather than by maximising sales. (Baker 1984)

The nodal point of the definitions, both of 'marketing' and 'the marketing concept', is the management of business activity with the ultimate customer in mind. However, both marketing as 'a practical, synthetic and applied discipline' (Baker 1984) and marketing as a concept have suffered from substantial criticism.

A number of studies have questioned the ability of marketing to guide companies through the minefield of new product development. Indeed, Lawton and Parasuraman (1980) examined the impact of adopting the marketing concept on new product development, concluding that there was very little impact at all. Bennett and Cooper (1981) cite a number of product innovations which have been the result of a technological breakthrough, a laboratory discovery or an invention, with only a vague notion of market need in mind.

Bell and Emory (1971) quote examples of other criticism levelled at the marketing concept, including the organisational stress and excessive costs brought about by its implementation. They raise the question of consumerism, pertinently asking why, if the marketing concept is working, there is a consumerist movement at all.

Perhaps the most perplexing aspect of the 'marketing concept' is the apparent difficulty experienced by those trying to implement it. The 'gap' between theory and practice seems to originate from the fact that practitioners do not see marketing as a means of solving their everyday business problems. Given the confusion over the definition of the marketing concept, this comes as no surprise. The intangible nature of the marketing concept has caused many theorists to avoid it, concentrating instead on techniques developed in its name.

> The over-riding impression that one gets from marketing periodicals and some marketing books is that technique is all-important. (King 1985)

> Marketing is — or ought to be — more than just a collection of functions and techniques. (Larreché 1985)

> The theorists talk of concepts, models, cycles, stages, criteria checklists, evaluations, the 4 ps and product portfolios. The practitioners talk their own individual language. (Kent 1984)

Consequently, when attempting to ascertain whether or not a company displays a marketing orientation, researchers often focus

MOUNT PLEASANT LIBRARY
TEL. 051 207 3581 Ext. 3701

on what Ames (1970) refers to as the 'trappings' of marketing: top management lip-service, the creation of a marketing department, transfer of product development and service functions to marketing, a strengthened advertising function, formal planning mechanisms and increased marketing expenditure. He goes on to explain that: 'these moves ... by themselves are no guarantee of marketing success. The kind of change that is needed is a fundamental shift in thinking and attitude throughout the company so that everyone in every functional area places paramount importance on being responsive to market needs' (Ames 1970).

In the same vein, Larreché describes real marketing as: 'an attitude of mind, a motivating force which runs through the company which continually challenges the established way of doing things. It should be the interface between the company and the whole world' (Larreché 1985).

It appears, then, that what the marketing concept calls for is more to do with an attitude of mind and company philosophy than with the detail of pricing and market research models (Bower 1985). This said, the transformation is not an easy one to make. In the words of Levitt: 'Corporations that have made the shift have found the process agonizing' (Levitt 1977).

All the more agonising, considering that theorists have yet to define clearly what marketing actually is and practitioners: 'tend not to define anything at all. They act first and give it a name afterwards. As a result there is a wide spread of activities which are called Marketing, and many of them seem to have failed' (King 1985).

Very recently a number of researchers have tried to go beyond the organisation of marketing within the company, placing less interest on marketing departments, directors, managers, administration and budgets. Instead they have focused on how marketing is actually carried out (Baker and Abou-Zeid 1982, Michaels 1982, Hooley, West and Lynch 1984, El Sahn 1984, Piercy 1985, and Spillard 1985). If the test of a philosophy is the result of its implementation, then what is required of research into marketing is an analysis of how marketing is actually carried out, rather than of the mechanisms and structures which may be mistaken for a true marketing orientation. A close inspection of the elements of 'real' marketing is the subject of the next section.

Many studies into business practice are carried out with a view to improving commercial performance in a given sphere of activity. For example, Frazier and Howell (1983) collected data from wholesalers of medical supplies and equipment to evaluate the impact on company performance of variations in business definition. Fredrickson (1984) studied the effect of a comprehensive strategic decision-making process on company performance, finding that strategic decision processes based on a rational model exhibited a strong positive relationship with average after-tax returns on assets.

On both sides of the Atlantic there is empirically based support for the notion that marketing increases business performance; Clifford and Cavanagh (1985) advise that, both strategically and tactically, customers' needs guide company operations. McBurnie and Clutterbuck (1988) have shown that successful companies have made marketing the linchpin of the organisation. While individual writers go some way to offering an explanation of what they mean by 'strategic marketing' or 'marketing techniques', it is difficult to find a comprehensive and orderly collection of the elements of marketing which are associated with superior business performance.

Baker and Abou Zeid (1982) identified three categories of marketing factors which proved to be important determinants of export success: attitudinal, strategic and tactical factors. Their categorisation provides a sound framework for discussing and analysing relevant literature which deals with the elements of marketing which enhance corporate performance.

Attitudinal Factors

Numerous authors describe marketing as a 'total company philosophy' (Ames 1970, Michaels 1982 and Larreché 1985):

> Adopting the marketing concept implies totally reorienting the whole company such that its strategic planning starts by identifying opportunities created by the potential for more effectively satisfying consumer wants. This then leads to the company's research, development engineering and production capabilities being aligned to developing a product and a marketing mix which optimally matches the prior identified opportunity in the market. (King 1985)

Clearly, espousal of the marketing concept involves a broad role for the marketing function within the organisation. R & D, engineering, design and finance departments should be infused with the spirit of marketing and the marketing department should interact with these.

Indeed, this kind of interface among company functions is thought to be instrumental to successful organisations. Hill (1985) examines the relationship between marketing and manufacturing functions, and shows how the choice of production methods and choice of markets and products are mutually dependent. Any mismatch between the exigencies of the market-place and manufacturing assets is therefore bound to affect the overall competitiveness of the firms. Similarly, Skinner (1980) highlights how important it is for manufacturing to contribute to the development of marketing strategy, so that the final strategy chosen can build on the company's manufacturing competences. Sir Kenneth Corfield, in his award-winning lecture in 1982, and Alexander (1985), drawing on empirical evidence, explain the importance of combining marketing and design functions to surmount the problems faced by British companies, a topic which recurs increasingly (Bonnet 1986, Takeuchi and Nonaka 1986 and Hart and Service 1988). Wilson (1984) suggests that one of the main reasons for Britain's comparative failure to convert invention into successful commercial innovation is 'the yawning gap' between those responsible for new product design and those who have to market the products. In a similar vein, Piercy (1985) found that in a sample of British companies, marketing personnel had virtually no control over two highly-rated critical success factors, namely new product development and pricing. Doyle's (1987) study also described the fact that only a little more than half of his sample companies' CEOs think in the long term about their markets.

There seems to be a consensus among researchers that the scope of 'marketing' is limited in British companies (Hayhurst and Wills 1972, Mann 1971, and Hooley *et al*. 1984). Further evidence of marketing's organisational isolation is the finding that in US companies, even sales and marketing are functionally distinct, with sales being seen as a line function and marketing as a staff responsibility (Webster 1981). That the 'profession of marketing' is not really a 'proper' profession is an attitude widely held by industrialists, politicians and the general public (King 1985).

Engineers, surveyors and accountants nearly all belong to professional 'closed shop' bodies, and while marketers do have professional associations they can join, many marketers do not belong to any professional association, and do not hold marketing qualifications.

This introduces the contentious area of marketing education and marketing training. Ames (1970) believes that those at the top responsible for marketing should be serious candidates for future general management jobs. The Centre for Interfirm Comparison (1978) reported the findings of a project carried out between 1974 and 1976, concluding that 'firms whose management teams possessed degrees or major professional qualifications generally had much better return on assets than other firms'. In a later study, the Centre found that firms where top management came from outside the firm and from outside the industry, did better generally than those firms whose sources were confined to their own firm or industry. In addition a formal training programme was seen to enhance overall company performance. Walsh and Roy (1983) found that firms planning to move 'up-market', which were, by and large, successful companies, had very definite views on the training of marketing personnel. They trained technically qualified people in marketing skills. It is, however, important to record the fact that marketing skills, qualifications and training can often be seen as the 'trappings' of marketing, rather than its 'substance', producing individuals with little or no aptitude for the job.

A further attitudinal issue is the authority bestowed upon the marketing department to carry out its functions. In a more general context, Project Sappho (Rothwell *et al*. 1974) — investigating which factors distinguish between successful and unsuccessful product introductions — found that where innovations were characterised by responsible individuals with greater seniority, new product development (NPD) was more successful. Piercy (1985) found that while, in general, chief marketing executives (CMEs) had status equal to production, accounting and sales executives, in approximately 15 per cent of the sample companies the status was lower. Three-quarters of marketing departments had some board representation — mostly restricted to one member in six — and the department of marketing was seen as being the most 'powerful department', rivalled most closely by finance. More recently, Doyle (1987) has shown that many UK companies are still financially driven with one in five top companies' CEOs defining their companies as financially oriented. To our knowledge, virtually no research has examined the precise link between the level of authority given to marketing in the company and the company's competitive performance. Webster (1981) laments the lack of senior executives with responsibility for marketing in US companies, labelling this as a 'cause for concern'. It is, however, intuitively attractive to support the proposition that if the marketing concept is to prevail throughout the company, then those primarily responsible for implementing it should be high-profile, senior people.

The final attitudinal issue is the way in which the company perceives the customer. Arguably the most telling factor in 'attitude', this is, predictably, the most elusive. To quote its primary source, a survey of the Queen's Award-winning companies for export achievement, Baker and Abou-Zeid (1982) define four areas for improving export performance which all centre on the *perception* of the customer:

- British manufacturers should view exporting as a basic activity which must not be dependent upon spare production capacity.
- British manufacturers should adopt a long-term approach to achieve profitability through satisfying buyers' needs.
- The idiosyncratic characteristics of foreign markets should be specifically addressed.
- British manufacturers need to pay attention to non-price factors when selling overseas.

Walsh and Roy (1983) describe the policies of successful companies who 'take pains to interact closely with their customers, participate in trade exhibitions and generally attempt to understand their market and the competition'. Taking specific examples of toy manufacturers, they relate the way in which Lego and Fisher-Price set about understanding their principal consumers: children. Fisher-Price runs a nursery for staff and local children, Lego uses the services of schoolchildren, and both employ child psychologists and people experienced in education to liaise with schools and nurseries. Alexander (1985) recounts the story of Servis, a company manufacturing washing machines that liaises with Procter and Gamble to gain a better understanding of the needs of the market. Saunders and Wong (1985), in their replication of *In Search of Excellence* (Peters and Waterman 1982), found that in successful companies, executives made significantly more sales calls and visits to customers' sites than did executives in less successful companies. In explaining Britain's apparent lack of commercial success, Wilson (1984) notes that while British companies are more likely to have market research managers and directors, and are prone to doing specific market research work for new product development, they tend to have less direct contact with their customers. While it is difficult to quantify 'perceptions of the customer', it is best described by the efforts made by a company to understand its markets in general.

These attitudinal factors have been addressed by writers both empirical and normative in their attempts to isolate what contributes to competitive success. Attention is now focused on the second set of factors: strategic factors.

Strategic Factors

'The output of strategic management is the development of corporate objectives and strategies for the total enterprise. This includes the definition of the firm's mission, its specific objectives, and strategies for achieving those objectives' (Kollat, Blackwell and Robeson 1972). As Brownlie (1985a) has summarised, the early stages of the 'Profit Impact of Market Strategies' (PIMS) project led the researchers to conclude that strategic planning makes a significant contribution to a firm's profitability. Some patchy evidence exists to support the contention that success in any given area of business activity is enhanced if a commitment to that area is made through the strategic output of the company. Walsh and Roy (1983), for example, found that companies who had won awards for design included an explicit commitment to good design in their corporate policies. Similarly, while relatively few studies have investigated UK exporting practice, those that have reveal that a commitment to establishing and sustaining long-term profitable relationships with customers in foreign markets is preferable to the myopic practice of maximising short-term profits by disposing of surplus finished stocks (ITI

Research 1978, Blood 1979, Baker 1979, Tookey 1969 and
McFarlane 1978). NEDO (1979) reported that a firm's goals can
fundamentally affect its ability and willingness to change, and
to accept new technology as a possible means of enhancing performance. It is therefore to be expected that success in marketing
is associated with a strategic commitment to the principles of the
marketing concept. An overview of the literature which allies
strategic marketing to successful performance reveals two main
areas of concern: the definition of company mission and the
nature of strategic plans and objectives.

(1) *Company Mission*

Company mission can be viewed as a long-term vision of what
the business is, or is striving to become. Answering the question
'What business are we in?' is based neither on tradition nor on
expectation, and in successful companies, defining the limits of
business is a fundamental activity, based on the requirements of
the market-place and the strengths of the firm. McKinsey (1983)
studied the characteristics of medium-sized growth companies
in the States and found that, among other things, successful companies reflect a strong sense of mission: that is, members of the
organisation have an 'unusually clear vision of the distinctive role
of the company'. Hooley and Lynch (1985) reported that in their
study of 1,504 British companies, the more successful ones, called
the 'high-fliers', displayed a higher strategic sensitivity and
responsiveness than the less successful group of companies,
called the 'also-rans'. The high-fliers were significantly more
likely to be active in growth markets. Such a strategic position
was not left to chance, but was seen by the authors to be a by-
product of their 'superior planning systems'. Similarly, Chaganti
and Chaganti (1983) compared the key features of the product
and market strategies of profitable and not-so-profitable small
businesses. One finding of the study, which involved 192 companies, was that the most profitable firms achieve this status by
identifying a niche in the market-place.
    In addition to empirical studies, which associate market defini-
tion with success, some normative writers also support this view.
South (1981), a corporate planning director at the Clark Equipment

Company, draws on experience to suggest that strategic competition is eking out a position of superiority by concentrating on specific market segments and offering differentiated products. Drawing on economic data and relevant articles at the time, both empirical and normative, Doyle (1985) concluded that a lack of commitment to marketing was a major cause of decline in British companies. He observed that the first step towards changing companies from a production or selling orientation to a marketing orientation involves the strategic planning process, which begins by identifying the opportunities created by the potential for satisfying consumer wants. More recent work by Doyle (1987) has hinted that managers are meeting the challenge of improving marketing effectiveness by radical approaches to new markets.

Cravens (1986) emphasises the need to understand an organisation's strategic situation as a starting point for developing a marketing strategy. He states that: 'strategic marketing decisions regarding the selection of market targets and positioning strategy (product, distribution, price, promotion) should be guided by the existing strategic situation and estimated future trends'. Commonly, the definition of product markets is a basic and important issue dealt with in marketing textbooks. Bell (1979), Kotler (1980) and Baker (1985) all deal with the strategic management process or marketing planning by beginning with the need for defining the business, the mission, or charter.

The overview given above does not seek to establish that definition of the company's product markets is the only prerequisite for business success. Nevertheless, both the fact that the topic is comprehensively dealt with in leading textbooks, and the few articles which *do* suggest some association between the two, indicate that it is a subject worthy of greater empirical attention.

(2) *Strategic Marketing Plans and Objectives*

In recent years there has been increasing attention given to the nature of corporate objectives and their influence on company performance. Specifically, concern has been growing over the apparent subjugation of long-term objectives by short-term profit maximisation, which has caused companies' marketing efforts to be undermined (Webster 1981 and Hayes and Abernathy 1980). Ames (1970) points out that formal annual speeches and reports declaring support for the marketing concept are useless in companies where management is reluctant to invest to achieve longer-term goals. He stresses that if marketing is to make a substantive contribution it needs 'breathing room'. In the UK, Baker and Abou-Zeid (1982) have underlined the need to make a long-term commitment to export markets, if success is to be achieved in exporting. In separating 'real marketing' from 'false marketing' King (1985) urges an approach which should 'work over time' while Hooley and Lynch (1985) note that high-flying companies recognise the need for long-range planning.

Saunders and Wong (1985) found that, on the whole, successful British companies were more oriented towards long-range planning than were less successful companies. Conversely, unsuccessful companies were significantly more concerned with returning good short-term profits. This study also revealed striking differences among actual objectives set by successful and unsuccessful companies. As can be seen from Table 4.1, successful companies' goals were far more aggressive than those of unsuccessful companies.

Unfortunately, our understanding of how strategic marketing planning and objectives influence company behaviour and performance is far from complete, resting as it does on a collection of normative articles and a handful of empirical findings. Gluck, Kaufmann and Walleck (1980) also suggest that a strategic emphasis, linking the rigour of formal planning to vigorous operational control, is the key to improving competitive performance.

Table 4.1 Targets and Strategies of Successful and Unsuccessful
           Companies

	Successful (%)	Unsuccessful (%)
Good short-term profits	53	85
Prevent decline	0	23
Defensive	0	23
Maintain position	24	15
Steady growth	41	31
Aggressive growth	24	8
Dominate market	11	0

Source: Saunders and Wong (1985).

Similarly, Karger and Malik (1975), Thune and House (1970) and Brownlie (1985b) conclude that strategic planning makes a significant contribution to company success. Day (1985), however, is more sceptical about the relationship between strategic planning and competitiveness. He contends that the actual implementation of the strategy may be more important than the strategy statement *per se*. While this is clearly true, what is unclear is whether the implementation of any strategy can take place without an explicit strategy formulation.

Also apparent is the fact that companies *do* experience difficulties in implementing strategic plans. Gray (1986) gives evidence of the problems encountered by companies in his sample. Although many were firmly committed to strategic planning, 87 per cent were frustrated and disappointed with their strategic planning system. Both Day and Gray emphasise the interdependency between strategic planning and the organisational implementation of strategic plans. The implementation of strategy is dependent upon the willingness and ability of production, sales, finance and other functions to work together. As Turnbull and Valla (1986) state, 'the necessity of high-level integration is, therefore, a prerequisite of efficient and effective strategic planning'.

Having reviewed both the attitudinal and strategic factors which might be expected to contribute to competitive success, the question of marketing tactics is now broached in an attempt to assess their contribution to competitive advantage.

Tactical Marketing Factors

Tactics are about taking decisions on a number of variables to influence the exchange of goods or services between the supplier and buyer. Typically, marketers have a number of tools they can use, and these are traditionally subsumed in the concept of the 4 Ps (McCarthy 1975). Unfortunately, the 4 Ps ignore key decisions that have to be made about markets. Determining where and to whom to sell is as important as decisions about the product, its price, and promotion. It is logical, therefore, that the marketing tactics associated with the selection of markets — namely market research and market segmentation — be included in the marketer's 'tool kit'. This section attempts to examine the impact of tactical marketing factors on competitive success by focusing on the findings of empirical research. The section is divided into 5 parts: (1) market research and market segmentation; (2) product policy; (3) sales and service policy; (4) promotional policy; and (5) pricing policy.

(1) *Market Research and Market Segmentation*

Researching the market is undertaken to gather information which aids a number of marketing decisions: the development of a new product, modification of an existing product, the content of advertising, pricing levels, etc. The 'effectiveness' of market research is often studied in relation to these specific decisions. Its importance as a marketing variable has been recognised for many years. In the early sixties a study undertaken by the National Industrial Conference Board revealed that first among eight causes of new product failure was inadequate market analysis (NICB 1964). A decade later, Project Sappho (Rothwell *et al*. 1974) revealed that failure in new product development was frequently accompanied by considerable neglect of the opinions of potential customers and no market research whatsoever.

Throughout the seventies market research was frequently associated with higher export performance (ITI Research 1979, British Institute of Management (BIM) 1975 and Rollason 1971). Such findings were confirmed in a recent study carried out by Baker and Abou-Zeid (1982), where 86 per cent of companies with a Queen's Award for export achievement carried out export market research. The most popular method of conducting market research was to use salesmen, while agents and government sources were less popular means of providing information. The major use to which the information was put was in selecting the foreign markets, while other uses were providing market information and identifying the required adaptation to suit the needs of these markets.

Cross-national comparisons have also highlighted the importance of market research to competitive success. For example, Connell (1979) describes how innovation in Japanese firms is typically initiated by sales and marketing personnel in the light of identified customer needs. This, along with other factors which emphasise customer interaction and interdepartmental co-operation in product development, distinguished Japanese firms from British firms.

Recent empirical work in the UK also lends weight to the argument that market research plays an important role in successful companies' marketing operations. Takeuchi and Quelch (1983) quote examples of successful companies who constantly monitor product quality from the buyers' point of view. The market research tactics involved include:

- conducting customer satisfaction surveys;
- tracking and recording all complaints and problems;
- having a questionnaire completed by all customers returning goods;
- carrying out extensive field tests on new products;
- analysing warranty claims;
- assessing the condition of goods received by administering a questionnaire.

Alexander (1985) shows that the use of qualitative market research by three companies (studied by her in some depth) generated information which was used to move beyond existing product concepts and to translate market requirements into innovative, successful designs. In the study by Walsh and Roy (1983), into the practices and policies of winners of the Design Council Awards, all award-winning companies paid attention to market research, and many ideas for new market opportunities, as well as design evaluation, came from market or customer research. Finally, Hooley and Lynch (1985) report that successful companies made much greater use of all types of market research than did less successful ones. Table 4.2 summarises the types of market research used by both High-fliers and Also-rans.

It is logical to hypothesise, in view of the above information, that market research has a positive influence on company performance. Given the dictate of the marketing concept — that the customer is the focus of the company — it is axiomatic that market research be included in the company's operations.

However, investigation of the existence and effectiveness of market research has been called into some question. Criticism by Ames (1970), Wilson (1984) and King (1985), among others, has emphasised that counting the number of heads in marketing

Table 4.2 Frequent Use of Market Research Techniques

	Sample	High Fliers	Also-rans	Significance
Sample size	1,504	175	1,329	'T'
Customer surveys	26.9%	33.7%	26.0%	0.05
Qualitative research	24.7%	30.9%	23.9%	0.0
Field experiments	18.5%	26.9%	17.4%	0.0
Laboratory experiments	12.4%	20.6%	11.3%	0.001

Source: Hooley and Lynch (1985).

research departments, or estimating market research budgets, focuses on the 'trappings' of marketing, not its 'substance'. Small low-budget research teams may be as effective in gaining an understanding of customers' needs, wants and perceptions as a larger organisation.

Webster (1981) views the hallmarks of the marketing concept as market segmentation and long-term strategic thinking, based on sound market information, and reports the difficulties experienced by top American managers in implementing them. Yet where market segmentation has been implemented, it appears to be associated with company success.

South (1981), Director of Clark Equipment Company, lists four factors which, from his experience, help to achieve competitive advantage, including 'concentrating on particular market segments' and 'offering products which differ from, rather than mirror, the competition'. He goes on to explain that 'the philosophy of blanket participation in all markets, products and technologies related to a business can give way to selective participation in those arenas with enough stability to ensure profitable return on investment'.

A more general view of the subject can be gained from the work of Chaganti and Chaganti (1983) who examined factors discriminating between successful and unsuccessful small companies. A major finding of the work was that the most profitable firms achieve this status by identifying and serving a niche in the market-place. Seller (1987) found that one distinguishing feature of a highly successful US beer company was its commitment to target marketing.

In the UK very little research has been carried out to evalua. the contribution of market segmentation and differentiate marketing (as opposed to mass selling) to competitive success. Recent work by Saunders and Wong (1985) suggests that successful companies 'create new product uses' and enter newly emerging segments to a significantly greater extent than unsuccessful companies. In contrast, unsuccessful companies enter significantly more established markets. Clearly, competitive companies pay greater attention to creating, selecting and focusing on segments where they perceive greater opportunity for differential advantage.

In conclusion, while much research exists which can help companies implement market research or segmentation strategies, relatively little work has been done which suggests how these two variables influence company performance, either in absolute terms, or in relation to other marketing factors.

(2) *Product Policy*

A number of writers have restated an easily forgotten truth: ultimately, company success is dependent upon its product policy (Baker 1985, Majaro 1977 and Borden 1963). 'Price' is the price of the product, 'advertising' is the advertising of the product, 'distribution' is the distribution of the product: all are product considerations (Kent 1984). NEDO (1977) published a study on non-price factors influencing export performance. Two major aspects were defined:

- Selling — including advertising, the effectiveness of agents and the degree of customer contact.
- Product — including design, reliability, specification, delivery and after-sales service.

This said, it is for the sake of clarity and concision of this chapter that product policy considerations are defined as those that have to do with physical characteristics: product quality, product modification, improvement and development.

Product Quality Articles, reports and research on product quality rarely work with identical definitions of quality. Connell (1979) considers quality to be an amalgamation of functional performance and functional suitability, design and reliability. Baker and Abou-Zeid (1982) perceive quality in terms of relative sophistication. Curry (1985) considers quality as a tool for product differentiation. Garvin (1984b) defines eight dimensions of quality: performance, features, reliability, conformance, durability, serviceability, aesthetics and perceived quality. The Task Force on Quality and Standards (NEDO 1985) reported to the NEDC that a 'quality product is defined as meeting identified market requirements of performance, reliability, and delivery and as being designed, developed and manufactured cost effectively and consistently, using the formalised disciplines of quality management techniques'.

In spite of semantic confusion over what 'product quality' comprises, some consensus can be found as to the role quality plays in achieving competitive success. Schoeffler, Buzzell and Heany (1974) rate product (or service) quality high on the list of factors influencing company profit performance. Particularly prolific in this field are the NEDC and various EDCs (NEDO 1982, 1983 and 1984). In addition to government bodies, Rothwell and Gardiner (1984), Garvin (1984a), the Centre for Interfirm Comparison (1978), Hooley and Lynch (1985), Saunders and Wong (1985), Ross and Shetty (1985) and Shetty (1987) all found that 'quality' is related to success. Normative writing has also urged the adoption of quality strategies (Ames, 1970, O'Cofaigh 1984 and Takeuchi and Quelch 1983).

A review of the literature reveals that issues pertaining to the elusive 'product quality' can be grouped as follows:

- Differentiation
- Design
- Performance
- Raw materials, components and manufacturing systems.

Differentiation   A differentiated strategy 'exists where the supplier seeks to supply a modified version of the basic product to each of the major sub-groups which comprise the basic markets' (*Macmillan Dictionary of Marketing and Advertising* 1984). A number of questions highlight the nature of product differentiation decisions (Avlonitis 1980):

- What are the boundaries beyond which no product should be added?

- How many different products should be offered in the line, and to what extent should they be differentiated?
- What is the number of different versions to be offered for each product line?
- What are the business characteristics that each product must meet to be included in the line?
- In how many segments should we compete in order to maintain a secure competitive position?

Saunders and Wong (1985) report that in their survey 53 per cent of excellent companies were 'good at product differentiation', while only 15 per cent of less successful companies were.

Porter's (1985) book on competitive advantage stresses the role of product differentiation. He outlines the sources of product differentiation which can be 'anywhere in the value chain': raw materials, technology developments, design differences, manufacturing specifications, reliability. However, he stresses that 'uniqueness' does not lead to differentiation or quality unless it is valuable to the potential customer. Related to this, interestingly, is the tale of Xerox, a company at one time overly concerned with one aspect of quality — the speed of copies. This attitude eclipsed the buyer's concern with the full cost of using the copier, and failed to be differentiated in a way meaningful to the buyer. Two ways of focusing on differentiation from the buyer's point of view are proposed: lower buyer's costs; increase buyer's performance. Porter's contention is that quality is developed to match buyer requirements and can create or enhance product differentiation and therefore competitive success. Again, the PIMS project (Schoeffler *et al.* 1974) underlines product differentiation (through innovation) among its nine influences which affect business success.

Design The Task Force on Quality and Standards (NEDO 1985) views design as an integral part of product quality. 'It is during the design stage that the manufacturing cost and quality objectives are set ...' The Task Force believes that design, quality assurance, standards and similar techniques are all part of the process of achieving customer satisfaction. Again, Saunders and Wong (1985) conclude that successful companies are 'stronger on design' than unsuccessful companies and this is echoed in the findings of Hooley and Lynch (1985) who report that high-flying companies are significantly more involved in product design than the also-rans. Walsh and Roy (1983) investigate two non-price product policy factors — design and innovation — defining design as 'fitness for use or function'.

A number of ways in which design-award-winning companies viewed the role of design in creating and sustaining competitive advantage are described. The product may be stronger, longer-lasting, better-looking, more reliable, made to a higher specification; it may allow the user to do something previously impossible; it may reduce customer costs, or reduce the price. In the award-winning companies, design was seen as a means of achieving superior product quality, which was an important objective in these companies, as some of their statements show:

'quality is more important than price'
'quality sells'
'durability is important'
'performance and design are important'
'we're not frightened to charge more for a good standard'
'we aim for technical excellence and forget profit'.

Rothwell and Gardiner (1984), in their paper 'The role of design in competitiveness', analyse the reasons why farmers purchased foreign or British goods for the period 1972–7. The 162 farmers who had bought British goods tended to cite 'price' as their principal motivation for buying British. In fact, out of eleven possible reasons for buying, design was ranked ninth, showing that the design of British agricultural equipment is not its main attraction. On the other hand, among the farmers who bought foreign machinery, design was the second most popular reason behind the choice. In general, all the non-price factors of reliability, design, performance and service were far more important than price to farmers buying foreign goods. The non-price factors considered important by those farmers buying British goods tended to relate to convenience rather than product quality. The authors conclude that the increasing penetration of the UK market has been associated with the high unit-value machines of high design excellence and high performance, a fact which is consolidated by the research findings quoted above. Findings such as these are echoed in many studies conducted by these researchers (Rothwell and Gardiner 1985 and Gardiner and Rothwell 1985).

In his article in *Management Today* (February 1985) Olins records the disastrous Chrysler European venture, associating the company's failure with its lack of commitment to and leadership in design. Chrysler, having acquired a number of ailing European companies, found that cars with unsuccessful product designs could not be uplifted merely by a change of name. However, a number of companies in various industries *do* succeed in making their products and services seem more desirable than those of their competitors — they can charge more for what is fundamentally the same, because they add value through design. Some examples include, in the industrial market: IBM, Olivetti and Apple, 3M; in consumer durables: Renault, BMW and Hoover; in retailing: Habitat, Benetton and Sainsburys — all are companies where design is well-coordinated and which occupy prime positions in their respective markets. Sciberras' (1979) study of international competitiveness and technical change in the US consumer electronic industry found that the difference in quality between Japanese and American companies largely rested on the former's commitment to design.

Since 1979, the Design Innovation Group, comprising the Open University and the University of Manchester Institute of Science and Technology, has been examining the role and contribution of design to competitiveness. It is impossible, within the scope of this chapter, to do justice to the breadth and depth of the group's work. This said, most findings indicate that companies who pay attention to how design can help deliver products that meet customer needs as well as reduce costs, and offer value for money, tend to fare better commercially than those that do not (Walsh and Roy 1985, Roy 1987, Bruce and Whitehead 1988). In addition, high performance companies have been found to integrate design skills with other business skills, echoing the work in the field of new product development (Snelson and Johne 1988, Cooper 1988 and Takeuchi and Nonaka 1986).

Performance The profusion of Economic Development Councils (EDCs) that have examined competition, both domestic and export, have nearly always included the functional performance of a product as a determinant of success. In 1979 the Machine Tool EDC reported that product performance was crucial to gaining competitive advantage. The NEDO (1965) study, 'Imported manufactures: an inquiry into competitiveness', showed that the technical performance, as perceived by the customer, was the primary reason for most imports of mechanical engineering products, electronic capital goods and scientific instruments. In a further study, Rothwell (1977) investigated the reasons why UK textile companies bought foreign machinery between 1970 and 1976. Most of the reasons given centred on the overall performance of the equipment, in terms of reliability, productivity and operational efficiency. (It is of course recognised that such features are often achieved through design, and the link between performance and design is therefore acknowledged.)

Piercy (1982) lists a number of key aspects in competitiveness which comprise the total package of values purchased by the customer: reliable delivery, short delivery lead time, service and marketing intangibles and product policy factors. Product policy factors are largely to do with reliability and performance, which should be aligned to customer requirements. In the study undertaken by Hooley and Lynch (1985), High-Fliers used product performance as a major emphasis in gaining new business to a far greater extent than Also-Rans.

Component parts, raw materials and manufacturing   The Task Force on Quality and Standards (NEDO 1985) states that 'the role of buyers in industry purchasing raw materials, components, subcontract work etc. is crucial to the achievement of quality, since poor quality materials cannot easily be manufactured into high quality goods'. Connell (1979) emphasises the value of component variety reduction in increasing the precision and reliability of products. He goes on to say that the realisation of such benefits calls for the ability and willingness to design and develop products around a narrower range of components.

Walsh and Roy's (1983) investigation into design of plastic products reveals that award-winning companies were committed to plastics and determined to enhance the buyer's perception of a material previously considered to be 'cheap and nasty'. Processing breakthroughs pioneered by several of these companies have since improved their commercial and design success, the most notable example being moulded polypropylene chairs. However, less design-conscious firms tended to design and process plastic products in essentially the same way as metal, ceramic or wood items. Porter (1985) notes the contribution of both raw materials and manufacturing systems in enhancing product quality.

Indeed, manufacturing systems and processes take their place in the array of factors contributing not only to product quality, but also to the general performance of the business. For example, the competitive edge that European and Japanese products have over their British equivalents in industries as diverse as textile machinery, colour televisions and personal computers, has been put down to the superior planning and control of their manufacturing process (Abernathy, Clark and Kantrow 1981). Hayes and Wheelwright (1984) and Parkinson (1986) argue that manufacturing is intrinsic to competitive success as it impinges on product development and customer satisfaction in both the *short*- and *long*-term.

The Task Force on Quality and Standards (NEDO 1985) stresses that the achievement of product quality requires up-to-date technical systems, information and management methods. This places responsibility for quality achievement on all concerned in product development, manufacture, procurement and related functions.

Product Modification, Improvement and Development   While product modification and development cannot be separated practically from the concept of product quality, it is a convenient way of disaggregating the vast and diverse literature on what product-related factors lead to business success. A number of studies have reinforced the axiom that product improvement and new product development are the lifeblood of companies. For example, the PEP (1964) observed that, in the main, firms attributed export success to 'better products', 'diversification of products', and 'new or more competitive lines'. In 1977 a NEDO report on printing and bookbinding machinery disclosed that the main reason for British manufacturers losing a share in the home market was a failure to introduce new products which were technically superior to competing products. (Other reasons pertinent to this study include: concentrating on engineering factors to the detriment of industrial design, with insufficient attention paid to detail; tardiness in adopting a market-oriented approach; inadequate contact with previous customers.) Baranson's (1980) study of the

Japanese challenge to US industry found that the relative success of Japanese firms is largely attributable to their strong commitment to commercialising new products along with their support of high risk, and acceptance of delayed return on investments.

The necessity of innovating, whether radically or incrementally, is widely recognised as being of critical importance, not only to a company but also to a nation (Baker 1985 and Kotler 1980). A number of studies examined the factors that enhance the success rate of new product development. While a detailed discussion of the many contributions in this field is beyond the scope of this chapter, a brief look at the more important pieces of research is in order. The Sappho Project (Rothwell *et al.* 1974), undertaken at the University of Sussex, revealed five key considerations distinguishing successful from unsuccessful innovation:

- Successful innovators have a much greater understanding of user needs.
- Successful innovators pay more attention to marketing and publicity.
- Successful innovators perform their development work more efficiently than less successful ones, but not necessarily more quickly.
- Successful innovators make more use of outside technology and scientific advice, not necessarily in general but in the specific area concerned.
- The responsible individuals in the successful attempts are usually of senior rank and have greater authority than in companies with less successful NPD programmes.

R.G. Cooper's (1979) project, New Prod, has defined 11 factors which discriminate between new product success and failure, and these are presented below in order of importance:

1. Introducing a unique — but superior — product.
2. Having market knowledge and marketing proficiency.
3. Having technical and production synergy and proficiency.
4. Avoiding dynamic markets with many new product introductions.
5. Being in a large, high-need growth market.
6. Avoiding the introduction of a high-priced product with no economic advantage.

7. Having good 'product/company fit managerial and marketing resources.
8. Avoiding a competitive market with sat
9. Avoiding products 'new to the firm'.
10. Having strong marketing communication effort.
11. Having a market-derived idea with consider ment involved.

More recently, research has focused on the need for integration of functional specialists at all stages of the NPD process (Tushman and Nadler 1986), linking this with the need for a speedy development process (Takeuchi and Nonaka 1986 and Johne and Snelson 1988). Indeed, discovering what factors distinguish successful NPD is a vast area of study in its own right, and cannot be fully covered here. However, central to the success of the new product programmes is 'adequate marketing' (Cooper 1979, Maidique and Zirger 1984, and Snelson and Johne 1988).

As previously mentioned, the separation of product modification and development from aspects of product quality — and also the subdivision of those factors that comprise product quality — is somewhat arbitrary, justified by the exigencies of clarity and simplicity. However, it is noteworthy that, to a very large extent, the many factors which comprise product policy (differentiation, design, performance, reliability, technological advancement, superior manufacturing, new product development, product modification, diversification, etc.) are interdependent ways of gaining competitive advantage and achieving success.

(3) *Sales and Service Policy*

In an assessment of marketing, King (1985) makes the point that: 'Real Marketing's starting point is designing a product or service to meet the wants of a group of customers. It is adding values to the raw materials to meet the totality of those wants, both physical and psychological. So it embraces suitability for purpose, quality, design, brand personality, style, availability, after sales service, ease of repair and all other aspects of a customer's relationship with a brand'. Clearly, the quality of a product can be

⎽anced by what Piercy (1982) calls 'marketing intangibles' and t is to these that we now turn.

A number of studies already mentioned have included 'service' on their list of factors distinguishing success from failure. In the list of strengths displayed by Japanese industry, Baranson (1980) included 'financial support' and 'after-sales service', where the latter included the redesign of parts and components and the upgrading or expansion of installed plant and equipment. The NEDO (1968) study, 'Market the World', reported that 90 per cent of the companies in the sample considered after-sales service and provision of spare parts to be vital to their export success. Heath *et al*. (1975) found that the ability to supply spares at short notice and after sales service were more important than price in the engineering industry. Brandt (1981), in a similar vein, explains that as a quick delivery is often crucial, companies who excel in this aspect of customer service usually display inventory holding and a backup organisation to deal with it. Takeuchi and Quelch (1983) describe the service guarantee that is provided by two leading American companies. This includes: stocking obsolete parts; 48-hour delivery anywhere in the world; and warranty and guarantee.

The authors suggest a useful list of questions which can help evaluate the level of service offered:

1) What are the companies' service objectives?
2) What services do they provide?
3) How do the companies' services compare with those of their competitors?
4) What services do the companies' customers want?
5) What is the customers' service demand pattern?
6) What trade-offs are the customers prepared to make?

Rothwell and Gardiner (1984), in their study of the buying criteria of 150 British farmers, found that 'speed of spares supply' was ranked third out of ten purchase criteria. In addition, those farmers who had bought foreign machinery in the period 1972–7 cited 'better service and spares supply' as the fourth most important reason for their choice, after reliability, design and performance.

Piercy (1982) divides 'service' into three areas, where each one improves the value of the product to the customer. *Commercial services* include physical distribution, which should be viewed as a way of adding value to the product for the customer, rather than just a matter of logistics. He argues that stockholding, transport methods used and the location of stock should all be decided in relation to the needs of the market, be they speed of delivery, sticking to delivery dates, meeting emergency orders, condition of goods on arrival, policy on returned goods, order-handling charges, or whatever. *Financial services* include credit terms, loans, the establishment of links with financial organisa-tions, publishing data on government aid for potential customers and tactics which facilitate the decision to buy. *Product support services* include pre-purchase advice and after-sales service. Such tasks introduce the role of the salesperson, who is often closest to the customer and in a position to give advice on product appli-cation, choice, storage, maintenance, grade and cost.

The sales team can often be a source of comparative advantage for a company: Piercy (1985) notes that one critical success factor in the sample companies was 'aggressive selling'; Webster (1981) laments the fact that too many MBA management teams are com-prised of people who are sales-averse; and Baker and Abou-Zeid (1982) show that in award-winning British companies, personal selling was the most widely used method of promotion. A great deal has been written regarding the comparative success of various selling styles and of various sales attributes. Complex models have been developed to aid the decisions central to the management of sales forces in the field, namely: allocating selling effort and setting sales force size; territorial design; sales forecasting; evaluation and control (Beswick and Cravens 1977). Sales volume is also seen to be a function of: environmental fac-tors; competition; company marketing strategy and tactics; salesforce organisation; and policies and procedures, i.e. organisa-tion, deployment of resources, recruiting and selection, training, rewards and incentives, evaluation and control (Walker, Churchill and Ford 1979, Ryans and Weinberg 1981, Avlonitis, Boyle and Kouremenos 1985). The literature is extremely fragmented and largely dominated by mathematical models which lack any managerial perspective; on the other hand, some studies examine the effect of attitudinal and other psychological variables on sales performances, but findings are difficult to verify in individual company settings (Cary 1976).

Personal selling is an important marketing tool which depends for its success on a number of points: organisation, training, remuneration and motivation, supervision and evaluation. While the complex and numerous issues that pertain to each point are beyond the scope of this text, their impact on the success of the firm should not be underestimated.

(4) *Sales Promotion and Advertising*

Broadly, sales promotion takes two forms: *above-the-line* and *below-the-line*. The line is an imaginary boundary between those advertising media which pay commission to advertising agencies and those which do not, the latter being 'below-the-line media'. The above-the-line media are: newspapers, magazines, television, radio, posters and cinema. Directories, yearbooks, matchbooks and point-of-sale materials (for example) are 'below-the-line'. (*Macmillan Dictionary of Marketing and Advertising* 1984.) Advertising has both an informative and persuasive role and, in this respect, can alter customer perceptions of the product. As Pickering (1976) suggests, advertising can increase brand loyalty, thereby decreasing price elasticity, through increased differentiation in the 'augmented product'. Bain (1956) suggests that advertising can have a cumulative and long-lasting effect and can be considered as a capital investment. Morrill (1970) has shown that advertising increases sales in industrial goods companies. Lehmann and Steckel (1985) examined the effect which advertising in trade directories has on calls made by sales people, and found that both the number of advertisements and the total area covered by the advertisements enhance sales coverage. The Advisor Study (Lilien 1979) revealed that a number of product and market variables — such as product sales rate, the stage of the product on its life-cycle curve, product complexity — affect the budgets of advertising and sales promotion.

Blasko and Patti (1984) compare the way in which companies, both consumer and industrial, set advertising budgets. They conclude that industrial companies have been slower than consumer companies to adopt advertising budgeting processes which have been made necessary by tighter economic conditions — namely, quantitative methods and the use of a percentage of anticipated sales. Conversely, the industrial companies relied to a significantly greater extent on the affordable and arbitrary approaches. The previously-mentioned NEDO (1965) report on mechanical engineering confirmed the expectation that higher export advertising budgets are associated with higher export sales. Similarly, the PEP (1964) survey revealed that the most important reason behind increased sales forwarded by companies was increased sales promotion. Slatter's (1977) study in the pharmaceutical industry reinforces the contention that promotion is a major explanation of increases in market share.

Sales promotion is a vast area of marketing in its own right, and therefore a few paragraphs cannot justly reflect the breadth of the literature on this subject which seeks to include advertising as a marketing tactic likely to affect the success of companies. However, perhaps the foregoing gives some indication of the issues at stake: the objectives and purposes of sales promotion; the choice of medium; and the method of budget allocation and promotional content.

(5) *Pricing Policy*

Most students of marketing are conversant with the theory that price is the means of achieving a balance between supply and demand. The concept says that the higher the price of a product or service, the less demand for it there will be, and vice versa. However, as can be seen from the array of other factors seen to influence company success in previous pages, price is not the only influence on demand. Nevertheless, in many of the studies previously mentioned, price was included on the list of *critical factors* which determine product success.

The Central Policy Review Staff (1975), for example, stressed that British car manufacturers must equalise their cost base to that of the competition if they are to achieve long-term viability. The Mechanical Engineering EDC (NEDO 1968) noted that, in order of importance, competition centred on price, delivery, credit terms, technical performance, after-sales service and repairs. A number of other articles report price as being the all-important factor: Atkin and Skinner (1975), for example, reveal that companies regard pricing policy as being either vital or most important to their achievements; and in 1980, Mikesell and Farah concluded that the decline of the US share of the markets in less-developed countries was mainly due to price factors. Rhys (1978), in seeking to explain the ills of the British car market, observed that quality improvements alone will not reverse the decline in market share because, at the end of the day, the trend of increased prices means that the consumer still has to pay more. Quality does not reduce the need for lower prices, but should shift the consumers' utility function upwards.

By contrast, a number of writers maintain that price is the least important determinant of demand: Posner and Steel (1979) contend that non-price factors are paramount in advanced manufacturing countries, and such a view is upheld by the studies of Kravis and Lipsey (1971), Udell (1964) and Patchford and Ford (1976). Evidently, there is great diversity of opinion with regard to the relative importance of price and non-price factors in determining the success of products and companies. A general view — drawn from many of the studies undertaken in this sphere — is that price is important if and when the quality of the rest of the package is comparable to the competition. Otherwise the cost benefit trade-off must be considered.

However, both types of competition are likely to differ in their effectiveness from industry to industry, market segment to market segment, product to product. In addition, the relative strengths of the competition and the cash flow situation of the company are also likely to affect the relative influence of price and non-price factors. Pricing, as an effective marketing tool, needs to have specific objectives. Lanzilloti (1978) has tabulated a number of common pricing objectives:

- pricing to achieve a target return on investment;
- stabilisation of price and margin;
- pricing to realise target market share;
- pricing to meet or prevent competition.

Once objectives have been established, a number of methods of setting prices are generally used:

- cost-plus pricing;
- matching competitive prices;
- marginal costing/contribution analysis;
- calculating a price that the market will bear.

While economists and academics tend to emphasise price factors, many researchers believe that non-price factors are more significant determinants of success. What is less clear, however, is how they fit into and influence the total package that is purchased by a customer.

4.4 Conclusions and Implications

The subject matter of this chapter has been the review of selected articles which examine the contribution of marketing to corporate competitiveness.

The material included in the review was classified under one of the following:

1. *Attitudinal* marketing factors which influence success.
2. *Strategic* marketing factors which influence success.
3. *Tactical* marketing factors which influence success.

Included in the first category were: (i) the involvement of functional departments in marketing decisions (and vice versa); (ii) the status of marketing in the company in its relative authority; and (iii) the broad perception of and approach to customers in the company. The second category of marketing factors involved: (i) the definition of the company's product markets (the 'Company Mission'); and (ii) the strategic plans and objectives of the company. The third and largest category focused on business practice and embraced: (i) market research and market segmentation; (ii) product policy (aspects of quality, NPD, product modification and improvement); (iii) service and sales policy; (iv) promotional policy and advertising; and (v) price policy.

While there has been some classification of these tactical issues to enhance the readability of the section, it is recognised that, in practice, many decisions relating to 'separate' issues are, in fact, interdependent. For example, the changes in price, advertising theme or target markets alter what is being offered to customers in return for their money and are therefore changes in the total package.

A number of general observations regarding the literature reviewed in this chapter are useful for defining the frontiers of our knowledge of the dimensions of marketing and corporate success:

1. While a number of suggestions have been made regarding

the *practical* nature of a 'marketing orientation', the majority
of writers have been content with a broad and general statement that a marketing orientation enhances success.

2. There is a tendency for many authors to focus solely on
    the organisational dimensions of marketing: the *trappings*
    rather than the *substance*.

3. Empirical work has often been concerned with only one
    or two factors and their effect on corporate success. This
    means that having carried out a literature review, a broad
    view is gained of how important the variable under con-
    sideration is to the success of the company, but no indica-
    tion is obtained of the relative importance of each variable
    in the total number of factors. A more comparative investi-
    gation of the variables would greatly improve knowledge
    in the area.

4. Empirical studies, where they have been undertaken, have
    often been confined to one industry, which limits the
    findings to the industry under investigation.

5. A large number of authors write normatively and this
    widens the gulf between theory and practice. That theorists
    and practitioners do not see some managerial issues in the
    same way is an indication of the work that needs to be done
    by researchers.

6. The various articles dealing with this subject have been
    written in different countries at different times and per-
    tain to the economic and social environments which existed
    at the time the study was executed. Such environments,
    in many cases, are no longer applicable to marketing in the
    eighties and nineties.

7. A number of key empirical studies have identified the
    characteristics of successful design companies, successful
    exporting companies, all-round successful companies, etc.,
    without attempting to verify if such characteristics are also
    present in less successful companies. Some progress
    towards defining what is *exclusive* to successful firms would
    consolidate findings which otherwise remain uncontested
    and unvalidated.

The next chapter describes two studies carried out at Strathclyde
which overcome the deficiencies of previous research in order to

come up with a clearer idea of what separates successful companies from unsuccessful ones.

References

Abernathy, W.J., Clark, K.B. and Kantrow, A.M. (1981) 'The new industrial competition', *Harvard Business Review*, September/October.

Alexander, M. (1985) 'Creative marketing and innovative consumer product decision — some case studies', *Design Studies*, vol. 6, no. 1, January.

Ames, B.C. (1970) 'Trappings versus substance in industrial marketing', *Harvard Business Review*, vol. 48, July/August.

Ansoff, I. (1968) *Corporate Strategy*, Penguin Books.

Argenti, J. (1978) *Systematic Corporate Planning*, Van Nostrand Reinhold (UK).

Atkin, B. and Skinner, R. (1975) *How British Industry Prices*, Industrial Market Research Ltd.

Avlonitis, G.J. (1980) *An Exploratory Investigation of the Product Elimination Decision-Making Process in the UK Engineering Industry*, University of Strathclyde, unpublished PhD thesis.

Avlonitis, G.J., Boyle, K.A. and Kouremenos, A.G. (1985) 'The relationship between selling styles and sales management practices: some evidence', *Proceedings of the Joint Annual Conference of the Marketing Education Group and the Academy of Marketing Science*, held at The University of Stirling, August.

Bain, J.S. (1956) *Price Theory*, John Wiley & Sons.

Baker, M.J. (1979) 'Export myopia', *Marketing*, vol. 9, no. 4, Spring.

Baker, M.J. (1985) *Marketing: An Introductory Text* (4th edn), Macmillan.

Baker, M.J. and Abou-Zeid, E.D. (1982) *Successful Exporting*, Westburn.

Baranson, J. (1980) *The Japanese Challenge to US Industry*, Lexington Books, D.C. Heath & Co.

Bell, M. (1979) *Marketing: Concepts and Strategy* (3rd edn), Houghton Mifflin.

Bell, M.L. and Emory, C.W. (1971) 'The faltering marketing concept', *Journal of Marketing*, vol. 35, October.

Bennett, R.C. and Cooper, R.G. (1981) 'The misuse of marketing: an American tragedy', *Business Horizons*, vol. 24, no. 6, November/December.

Bennis, W. and Nanus, B. (1985) *Leaders: The Strategies for Taking Charge*, Harper and Row.

Beswick, C.A. and Cravens, D.W. (1977) 'A multi-stage decision model for sales force management', *Journal of Marketing Research*, May.

Blasko, C. and Patti, F. (1984) 'The advertising budgeting practices of industrial marketers', *Journal of Marketing*, vol. 48, Fall.

Blood, P. (1979) 'Britain's amateur marketers', *Marketing*, January.

Bonnet, D.C.L. (1986) 'The nature of the R & D/Marketing cooperation in the design of technologically advanced new industrial products', *R & D Management*, vol. 16, no. 2.

Borden, N.H. (1963) 'The growing problem of product line planning' in C.J. Dirksen, A. Kroger and L.C. Lockley (eds), *Readings in Marketing*, R.D. Irwin.

Bower, J. (1985) Quoted in 'The complexities that often lead to failure', by C. Lorenz, *The Financial Times*, Wednesday, 17 April.

Boynton, A.C. and Zmud, R. (1984) 'An assessment of critical success factors', *Sloan Management Review*, Summer.

Brandt, S.C. (1981) 'Beyond planning', Section Three in *Strategic Planning In Emerging Companies*, Addison-Wesley.

British Institute of Management (BIM) (1975) *Managing the Export Function: Policies and Practices in the Small and Medium Company*, Survey Report No. 26.

Brownlie, D. (1985a) 'The anatomy of strategic marketing planning', *Journal of Marketing Management*, vol. 1, no. 1, Summer, pp. 35–63.

Brownlie, D. (1985b) 'Strategic marketing concepts and models' *Journal of Marketing Management*, vol. 1, no. 2, Winter, pp. 157–194.

Bruce, M. and Whitehead, M. (1988) 'Putting design into the picture: the role of product design in consumer behaviour', *Journal of Market Research Society*, vol. 30, no. 2.

Burns, T. and Stalker, C.M. (1961) *The Management of Innovation*, Tavistock Publications.

Buzzell, R. and Gale, B. (1974) 'Market share — a key to profitability' *Harvard Business Review*, January/February, pp. 97–106.

Cary, F.T. (1976) 'IBM's "Guidelines to Employee Privacy" ', *Harvard Business Review*, vol. 54, September/October.

Central Policy Review Staff, The (1975) *The Future of the British Car Industry*, HMSO.

Central Statistical Office (1985) *The Monthly Digest of Statistics*, HMSO, October.

Centre for Interfirm Comparison, The (1978) *Management Policies and Practices and Business Performance — Some Additional Research (Project 1A)*, The Centre for Interfirm Comparison, September.

Chaganti, R. and Chaganti, R. (1983) 'A profile of profitable and not so profitable small businesses', *Journal of Small Business Management*, July.

Channon, D.F. (1973) *Strategy and Structure of British Enterprise*, quoted in D.E. Hussey 'Strategic management: lessons from success and failure', *Long Range Planning*, vol. 17, no. 1.

Clifford, D.K. and Cavanagh, R.E. (1985) *The Winning Performance: How America's High-Growth Midsized Companies Succeed*, Sidgwick and Jackson.

Connell, D. (1979) *The UK's Performance in Export Markets: Some Evidence from International Trade Data*. Discussion Paper 6, NEDO.

Cooper, R.G. (1979) 'The dimensions of industrial new product success and failure', *Journal of Marketing*, vol. 43, Summer.

Cooper, R.G. (1988) 'The new product process: a decision guide for managers', *Journal of Marketing Management*, vol. 3, no. 3.

Corfield, Sir K. (1982) 'No man is an island — design in context', SIAD/Maurice Hill Award Lecture.

Cravens, D.W. (1986) 'Strategic forces affecting marketing strategy', *Business Horizons*, September/October.

Crosier, K. (1975) 'What exactly is marketing?' *Quarterly Review of Marketing*, Winter.

Curry, D.J. (1985) 'Measuring price and quality competition', *Journal of Marketing*, vol. 49, Spring.

Day, G. (1985) 'Tough questions for developing strategies', *The Journal of Business Strategy*, vol. 6, no. 2.

Doyle, P. (1985) 'Marketing and the competitive performance of British industry: areas for research', *Journal of Marketing Management*, vol. 1, no. 1, Summer.

Doyle, P. (1987) 'Marketing and the British chief executive', *Journal of Marketing Management*, vol. 3, no. 2, Winter.

Doyle, P., Saunders, J. and Wong, V.C. (1985) *A Competitive Investigation of Japanese Marketing Strategies in the British Market*, Report to ESRC.

Dunn, M.G., Norburn, D. and Birley, S. (1985) 'Corporate culture: a positive correlate with marketing effectiveness', *International Journal of Advertising*, vol. 4, pp. 65–73.

Eastlack, J.B. and McDonald, P.R. (1970) 'CEO's role in corporate growth', *Harvard Business Review*, vol. 48, May/June, pp. 150–63.

El Sahn, M.F.F. (1984) *The Marketing of Financial Services: An Exploration of the Application of Marketing Concepts and Policies to Scottish Banks*, unpublished Ph.D. thesis, Department of Marketing, University of Strathclyde.

Emery, F.E. and Trist, E.L. (1965) 'The causal texture of organisational environments', *Human Relations*, 18 February, pp. 21–32.

Fraser of Allander Institute (1986) *The British Economy*, Fraser of Allander Institute, vol. 11, no. 3, February.

Frazier, G.L. and Howell, R.D. (1983) 'Business definitions and performance', *Journal of Marketing*, vol. 47, Spring.

Fredrickson, J.W. (1984) 'The comprehensiveness of strategic decision processes: extension, observation and future direction', *Academy of Management Journal*, vol. 27, no. 3.

Gagliardi, P. (1986) 'The creation and change of organisational cultures', *Organization Studies*, vol. 7, no. 2.

Gardiner, P. and Rothwell, R. (1985) 'Tough customers: good designs', *Design Studies*, vol. 6, no. 1, January.

Garvin, D. (1984a) 'Product quality: an important strategic weapon', *Business Horizons*, vol. 27, no. 3, March/April.

Garvin, D. (1984b) 'What does product quality really mean?', *Sloan Management Review*, vol. 26, no. 1, Fall.

Gluck, W.F., Kaufmann S.P. and Walleck, A.S. (1980) 'Strategic management for competitive advantage', *Harvard Business Review*, July/August.

Goldsmith, W. and Clutterbuck, D. (1984) *The Winning Streak, Britain's Top Companies Reveal Their Formulas for Success,* Weidenfeld & Nicolson.

Gray, D.M. (1986) 'Uses and misuses of strategic planning', *Harvard Business Review,* January/February.

Halbert, M. (1965) Quoted in M.J. Baker (1984) *Dictionary of Marketing and Advertising,* Macmillan.

Hamermesh, R.G., Anderson, M.J. and Harris, J.E. (1978) 'Strategies for low market share businesses', *Harvard Business Review,* May/June.

Hart, S.J. and Service, L.M. (1988) 'The effect of managerial attitudes to design on company performance', *Journal of Marketing Management,* vol. 4, no. 2.

Hayes, R. and Abernathy, W. (1980) 'Managing our way to economic decline', *Harvard Business Review,* July/August.

Hayes, R.H. and Wheelwright, S.C. (1984) *Restoring our Competitive Edge,* John Wiley & Sons.

Hayhurst, R. and Wills, G. (1972) *Organisational Design for Marketing Futures,* Allen & Unwin.

Heath, J.B. *et al.* (1975) *A Study of the Evaluation of Concentration in the Mechanical Engineering Sector for the United Kingdom,* Commission of the European Communities, October.

Hill, T. (1985) *Manufacturing Strategy,* Macmillan.

Hooley, G.J. and Lynch, J. (1985) 'Marketing lessons from UK's high-flying companies', *Journal of Marketing Management,* vol. 1, no. 1, Summer.

Hooley, G.J., West, C.J. and Lynch, J.E. (1984) *Marketing in the UK: A Survey of Current Practices and Performance,* The Institute of Marketing.

ICC *Business Performance Analysis,* 1986/87 and 1987/88 editions, ICC Information Group, London.

ITI Research Ltd (1978) A study conducted by ITI Research on behalf of the Royal Society of Arts, mentioned by J. Pointon in 'The information needs of exporters', *Marketing,* July.

ITI Research Ltd (1979) *The Barclays Bank Report on Export Development in France, Germany and the United Kingdom,* Barclays Bank International.

Johne, F.A. and Snelson, P.A. (1988) 'Marketing's role in successful new product development', *Journal of Marketing Management,* vol. 3, no. 3, Spring.

Kanter, R.M. (1983) *The Change Masters: Corporate Entrepreneurs at Work,* Allen & Unwin.

Karger, P.W. and Malik, Z.A. (1975) 'Long range planning and organisational performance', *Long Range Planning,* December.

Kent, R. (1984) *Marketing Faith and Marketing Practice: A Study of Product Range in the Scottish Food Processing Industry,* unpublished MSc thesis, Department of Marketing, University of Strathclyde.

Khandwalla, P.N. (1977) *The Design of Organisations,* Harvard Press.

King, S. (1985) 'Has marketing failed or was it never really tried?', *Journal of Marketing Management,* vol. 1, no. 1, Summer.

Kollat, D.T., Blackwell, R.D. and Robeson, J.F. (1972) *Strategic Marketing,* Holt, Rinehart & Winston.

Kotler, P. (1980) *Marketing Management Analysis, Planning and Control* (4th edn), Prentice-Hall.

Kravis, B. and Lipsey, R.E. (1971) *Price Competitiveness in World Trade*, National Bureau of Economic Research.

Lanzilloti, F. (1978) 'Pricing objectives in large companies', *American Economic Review*, December.

Larreché, J.C. (1985) Quoted in 'Late converts to the gospel of marketing' and 'The complexities that often lead to failure,' by C. Lorenz, *Financial Times*, Wednesday, April 17.

Lawton, L. and Parasuraman, A. (1980) 'The impact of the marketing concept on new product planning', *Journal of Marketing*, Winter.

Lehmann, D.R. and Steckel, J.H. (1985) 'Effective advertising in industrial supplier directories', *Industrial Marketing Management*, vol. 14.

Levitt, T. (1977) 'Marketing when things change', *Harvard Business Review*, November/December.

Lilien, G.L. (1979) 'Advisor 2: modelling the marketing mix decisions for industrial products', *Management Science*, vol. 23, no. 2, February.

McBurnie, A. and Clutterbuck, D. (1988) *The Marketing Edge*, Penguin Business Books.

McCarthy, E.J. (1975) *Basic Marketing* (5th edn), Irwin.

McFarlane, G. (1978) 'Scots Queen's Award winners don't excel', *Marketing*, April.

McKinsey and Co. (1983) *The Winning Performance of the Midsized Growth Companies*, American Business Conference, May, McKinsey and Co., London.

Macmillan Dictionary of Marketing and Advertising (1984) edited by M.J. Baker, Macmillan.

Maidique, M.A. and Zirger, B.J. (1984) 'A study of success and failure in product innovation — the case of the US electronics industry', *IEEE Transactions on Engineering Management*, 23 August.

Majaro, S. (1977) *International Marketing: A Strategic Approach to World Markets*, George Allen & Unwin.

Mann, J. (1971) 'Natural and effective status of chief marketing executives in Yorkshire industry', in G. Wills (ed.) *Exploration in Marketing Thought*, Crosby Lockwood.

Marlow, H. (1984) *Success*, Institute of Personnel Management.

Matthews, R. (1985) *Managing for Success*, CBI, London.

Michaels, E.G. (1982) 'Marketing muscle', *Business Horizons*, May/June.

Mikesell, R.F. and Farah, M.G. (1980) *US Export Competitiveness in Manufactures in the Third World Markets*, The Centre for Strategic and International Studies, Georgetown University.

Morrill, J.E. (1970) 'Industrial Advertising Pays Off', *Harvard Business Review*, March/April.

Muhlbacher, H., Vyslozil, W. and Ritter, A. (1987) 'Successful implementation of new market strategies — corporate culture perspective' *Journal of Marketing Management*, vol. 3, no. 2.

National Industrial Conference Board (NICB) (1964) *Why Products Fail*, Conference Board Record.

NEDO (1965) *Imported Manufactures, An Enquiry into Competitiveness*, NEDO.

NEDO (1968) *Market the World: A Study of Successful Exporting*, A report of a working party of the Economic Development Committee for the mechanical engineering industry, NEDO.

NEDO (1974) *Mechanical Engineering*, NEDO.

NEDO (1976) *The UK and West German Manufacturing Industry 1959–1972*, NEDO.

NEDO (1977) *The UK Printing and Bookbinding Machinery Industry: Market Prospects to 1980*, Printing and Bookbinding Machinery SWP.

NEDO (1979) *A Financial Study of British Machine Tool Companies*, Machine Tool EDC.

NEDO (1981) *Industrial Performance, Trade Performance and Marketing*, EDC/SWP, August.

NEDO (1982) *Policy for the UK Electronics Industry*, NEDO.

NEDO (1983) *Standards Quality and Competitiveness*, A report of the conference, May, NEDO.

NEDO (1984) *Improving Performance in the Manufacture of Fully Fashioned Outerwear*, Knitting EDC.

NEDO (1985) *Quality and Value for Money*, A report to the National Economic Development Council by the Task Force on Quality and Standards, NEDO, May.

Neghandi, A. and Reimann, B. (1973) 'Task environment, decentralisation, and organisational effectiveness', *Human Relations*, 26 May, pp. 203–14.

Oakley, J. (1984) *Managing Product Design*, Weidenfeld & Nicolson.

Oakley, M. (1985) 'The influence of design on industrial and economic achievement', *Managerial Decisions*, vol. 23, no. 4.

O'Cofaigh, T.F. (1984) 'Competitiveness, monetary policy and economic development', *Central Bank of Ireland Annual Report*, January.

Olins, W. (1985) 'Management by design', *Management Decision*, February.

Parkinson, S.T. (1986) 'Niche marketing and manufacturing strategy', Proceedings of the 19th Annual Conference of the Marketing Education Group, Plymouth, July.

Patchford, B.T. and Ford, G.T. (1976) 'A study of prices and market share in the computer mainframe industry', *Journal of Business*, April.

PEP (1964) 'Firms and their exports', *Planning*, vol. XXX, November.

Peters, T.J. and Austin, N. (1986) *A Passion for Excellence*, Fontana.

Peters, T.J. and Waterman, R.W. (1982) *In Search of Excellence*, Harper & Row.

Pickering, J.F. (1976) *Industrial Structure and Market Conduct*, Robertson & Co.

Piercy, N. (1982) *Export Strategy: Markets and Competition*, George, Allen & Unwin.

Piercy, N. (1985) 'The role and function of the chief marketing executive and the marketing department — a study of medium-sized companies in the UK', *Journal of Marketing Management*, vol. 1, no. 3, Spring.

Porter, M.E. (1980) *Competitive Strategy: The Techniques for Analysing Industries and Competitors*, The Free Press.

Porter, M.E. (1985) *Competitive Advantage: Creating and Sustaining Superior Performance*, The Free Press.

Posner, M. and Steel, A. (1979) 'Price competitiveness and performance of manufacturing industry', in F. Blackaby (ed.) *De-Industrialisation*, Heineman Educational Books.

Rhys, D.G. (1978) 'Car market price competition in the mid 1970s', *Management Decision*, vol. 16, no. 4.

Rollason, B. (1971) 'What the successful exporter knows', *Marketing*, November.

Ross, J.E. and Shetty, Y.K. (1985) 'Making quality a fundamental part of strategy', *Long Range Planning*, vol. 18, no. 1.

Rothwell, R. (1977) 'The Role of Technological Change in International Competitiveness: The Case of the Textile Machinery Industry', *Management Decision*, vol. 15, no. 6.

Rothwell, R. *et al.* (1974) 'Project SAPPHO updated — Project SAPPHO Phase II', *Research Policy*, 3.

Rothwell, R. and Gardiner, P. (1984) 'The role of design in competitiveness', in R. Langdon, *Design and Industry*, Proceedings of the Design and Industry Section of an international conference on design policy held at the Royal College of Art, 20—23 July 1982.

Rothwell, R. and Gardiner, P. (1985) 'Invention, innovation, re-innovation, and the role of the user: a case study of British Hovercraft Development', *Technovation*, 3.

Roy, R. (1987) 'Design for business success', *Engineering*, January.

Ryans, A.B. and Weinberg, C.B. (1981) 'Sales force management: integrating research advances', *California Management Review*, vol. XXIV, no. 1, Fall.

Saunders, J. (1987) 'Attitudes, structure and behaviour in a successful company', *Journal of Marketing Management*, vol. 3, no. 3, Winter.

Saunders, J. and Wong, V. (1985) 'In search of excellence in the UK', *Journal of Marketing Management*, vol. 1, no. 2, Winter.

Schoeffler, S., Buzzell, R.D. and Heany, D.F. (1974) 'Impact of strategic planning on profit performance', *Harvard Business Review*, March/April, pp. 137—45.

Sciberras, E. (1979) *International Competitiveness and Technical Change: A Study of US Consumer Electronic Industry*, Science Policy Research Unit, September.

Seller, P. (1987) 'How Busch wins in a dodgy market', *Fortune*, 22 June.

Shetty, Y.K. (1987) 'Product quality and competitive strategy', *Business Horizons*, May/June.

Skinner, W. (1980) 'Manufacturing missing link in corporate strategy', *Harvard Business Review*, May/June.

Slatter, S.P. (1977) *Competition in the Pharmaceutical Industry*, Croom Helm.

Snelson, P.A. and Johne, F.A. (1988) 'Product development practices in large US and UK firms', *Proceedings of the 17th Annual Conference of the European Marketing Academy*, April, Bradford.

South, S.E. (1981) 'Competitive advantage: the cornerstone of strategic thinking', *Journal of Business Strategy*, vol. 1, no. 4, Spring.

Spillard, P. (1985) *Organisation and Marketing*, Croom Helm.

Takeuchi, H. and Nonaka, I. (1986) 'The new product development game', *Harvard Business Review*, January/February.

Takeuchi, H. and Quelch, J.A. (1983) 'Quality is more than making a good product', *Harvard Business Review*, vol. 61, no. 4, July/August.

Thune, S.S. and House, P.S. (1970) 'Where long range planning pays off', *Business Horizons*, August.

Tookey, D.A. (1969) 'International business and political geography', *British Journal of Marketing*, Autumn.

Turnbull, P.W. and Valla, J.P. (1986) 'Strategic planning in industrial marketing: an interaction approach', *European Journal of Marketing*, vol. 20, no. 7.

Tushman, M.L. and Nadler, D.A. (1986) 'Organizing for innovation', *California Management Review*, vol. XXVIII, no. 3.

Udell, J. (1964) 'How important is pricing in competitive strategy?', *Journal of Marketing*, January.

Vaill, B.P. (1982) 'The purposing of high-performing systems', *Organisational Dynamics*, Autumn.

Varadarajan, P.R. (1986) 'Product diversity and firm performance: an empirical investigation', *Journal of Marketing*, 50, July.

Walker, O.C., Churchill, C.A. and Ford, N.M. (1979) 'Predicting a salesperson's job effort and performance: theoretical, empirical and methodological considerations in sales management; new developments from behavioural and decision model research', *AMA and MSI Conference Proceedings*, August.

Walsh, V. and Roy, R. (1983) *Plastics Products: Good Design, Innovation and Business Success*, The Open University, Design Innovation Group DIG-01, August.

Walsh, V. and Roy, R. (1985) 'The designer as "gatekeeper" in manufacturing industry', *Design Studies*, vol. 6, no. 3.

Webster, F.E. (1981) 'Top management's concerns about marketing: issue for the 1980s', *Journal of Marketing*, Summer.

Wilkins, A.L. and Ouchi, W.G. (1983) 'Efficient cultures: exploring the relationship between culture and organisational performance', *Administrative Science Quarterly*, vol. 28.

Wilson, A. (1984) 'Innovation in the marketplace', *Management Today*, June.

5
Second Opinions

The previous chapter reviewed recent research and thinking regarding the impact of marketing on the commercial success of a company. Also highlighted were a number of limitations concerning the conceptual bases and research methods used by researchers in the field to discover what contributes to competitiveness. Arguably, the most serious of these limitations are: over-generalisations, in both normative and descriptive work, about 'marketing orientation' being a prerequisite for success, and a concomitant lack of precision regarding *how* this marketing orientation may be manifested and implemented within a firm; empirical studies which are confined to one industry (or one type of industry), which results in uncertainty as to whether findings can be generalised to cover a broader base of industries; a single-factor focus in most research studies which leads to an incomplete understanding of the relative importance of factors influencing business success; and assumptions that features common to a number of successful companies explain their commercial performance, without checking to see if these features are absent from firms that are less successful.

In order to consolidate knowledge of the scope and nature of marketing factors that distinguish between successful and unsuccessful companies, two separate, but related, studies were carried out at Strathclyde University's Marketing Department: *Project MACS* ('Marketing and Competitive Success'), funded by the ESRC (Economic and Social Research Council) and the Institute of Marketing, and *Profit by Design*, funded by the Design Council, Scotland. The purpose of this chapter is to describe the precise objectives of, and the research methods employed by, these two studies.

5.1 Project MACS

The overall aim of Project MACS was to assess trends in current thinking about the contribution of marketing to business success, and then to design a study to test the foundations of these trends. This would provide the basis for making *sound* and *proven* recommendations for improving competitive performance.

As mentioned above, to impute commercial success to marketing factors alone is unsatisfactory, given that the explanations of company performance are likely to be manifold and overlapping. (See Figure 4.1 in Chapter 4). It follows, then, that to look at only one of the five constructs depicted by Figure 4.1 will yield an inadequate explanation. A partial solution to this problem is presented by the considerable interconnection among these constructs or 'sets', in that it is possible to look at the elements of one construct through the elements of another. By way of example: in a study of organisational culture by Dunn, Norburn and Birley (1985), one aspect identified as having considerable impact on performance was a shared belief in informal communication. In this case, the *culture* of the organisation was manifested, in part, through the *style* of its managers. Potentially, researchers could investigate any one of these factors from the viewpoint of another. There is, however, a compelling argument for selecting marketing as *the* medium through which to study competitive success. Since marketing is defined as part of a company's total philosophy, manifested as a strategic focus on the environment as well as a business function, it should be detectable in the organisational, strategic and managerial factors in Figure 4.1. (Bradley 1986).

The approach taken by Project MACS is based upon this reasoning and it triggered the development of a conceptual framework designed to investigate systematically the relative contribution of marketing factors to company success. This framework includes several factors subsumed by the five constructs shown in Figure 4.1, and it examines them from a marketing perspective. It contains three elements: strategic marketing factors, tactical marketing factors and business or company performance, which, along with the factors contained within them, are derived from the literature review in the previous chapter (see Figure 5.1).

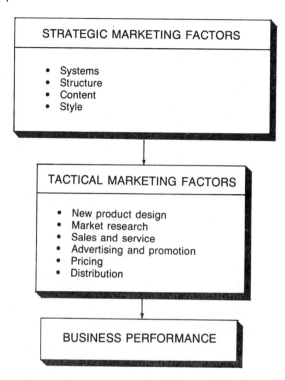

Figure 5.1 A Conceptual Framework for Project MACS

The first two elements in Figure 5.1 — strategic marketing factors and tactical marketing factors — are the independent variables, while the third — business performance — is the dependent variable. In order to identify which of the independent variables are associated with success, the data collected had to be both descriptive and explanatory, and the design had to be comparative. These conditions led to the following specific research objectives:

1. To describe and compare the contribution of strategic decision-making in both successful and less successful companies.
2. To describe and compare the nature of the strategic decision-making process in both groups of companies.

3. To describe and compare those issues relevant to strategic
    planning in both groups.
4. To describe and compare tactical aspects of marketing
    behaviour in successful and unsuccessful companies (this
    includes quality standards and control; new product
    development; methods and sources for gathering market
    information; market segmentation; service and after-sales
    provision; distribution, advertising and pricing).

In order to meet these objectives a research design which would
compare successful and less successful companies was developed
and implemented in both above- and below-average sectors of
the economy. How these sectors were identified is described
below.

The Nature and Measurement of Company Success

Many studies into business practice are carried out with a view
to improving commercial performance in a given sphere of
activity. For example, Frazier and Howell (1983) collected data
from wholesalers of medical supplies and equipment to evaluate
the impact of variations in business definition on company performance. Fredrickson (1984) studied the effect of a comprehensive strategic decision-making process on company performance,
finding that strategic decision processes based on a rational model
exhibited a strong positive relationship with average after-tax
returns on assets.

Success has many dimensions. At the simplest level it may be
viewed as the consistent achievement of company objectives,
which can vary from a definition of the role the company seeks
to play in its selected industry to targets related to innovation and
technology. It is, however, a common view that the most usual
type of company objective is finance-related — for example, sales
volume, market share, return on investment (Bell 1979 and Kotler
1980). Indeed, publications like *Times 1000*, *Fortune 500* and the
Scottish Business Insider, which all rank companies in terms of their
performance, use financial measures such as annual turnover,
pre-tax profit, share prices and return on shareholders' funds.
The majority of studies designed to test what it is that

distinguishes successful companies have all used financial criteria as measures of successful performance. Carter and Williams (1957) used three criteria to define successful performance: trading profits as a percentage of fixed assets and stock for the average of 2 recent years; trading profits for the 4 previous years as a percentage of the 4 years prior to those; and increase of net tangible assets for the 6 previous years as a percentage of the net tangible assets for the median year. Reece and Cool (1978), in a special report on measuring performance, consider return on investment to be the most popular measure, where companies use financial reporting methods involving investment centres.

Ferguson and Dickenson (1981) believe that performance should be measured in terms of how an organisation should manage its critical success factors (CSF). Five proposed CSFs are:

- Can the company cope with inflation?
- Will adequate financial resources be available?
- Is the company positioned to be competitive?
- Does the company have a strategy for corporate planning?
- Will adequate financial resources be available?

Peters and Waterman (1982) use seven criteria to define excellent company performance: three measure growth and long-term wealth creation over a twenty-year period; three relate to return on capital and sales; and the seventh performance measure is based on the company's history of innovativeness. Goldsmith and Clutterbuck (1984) define successful companies using 3 criteria: high growth in assets, turnover and profit over the past 10 years; a consistent reputation within the industrial sector as a leader; and a good solid public reputation.

The Appendix to this chapter gives a more complete picture of the types of financial measurement of performance that have been used by researchers. Each measure is listed in order of priority, according to the number of researchers (who took part in this survey) that use it. The most popular in each section are: gross sales, return on investment, return on capital employed, return on equity and compound asset growth. While a complete review of the merits and demerits of each type of measurement is beyond the scope of this chapter, it is useful to summarise the major conditions that measurement criteria should meet (NEDO

1976, ICC 1986, Reece and Cool 1978, Argenti 1978 and Karger and Malik 1975).

First, it is helpful if the measure can be verified from published sources, to minimise the effects of respondents' errors and to simplify the research questionnaire. Second, where industries are to be compared, the measure should not vary from one industry to another. Third, the measures should vary as little as possible from company to company, and should not be readily manipulated by different accounting conventions. Finally, it is helpful to have measures which can be calculated and compared longitudinally.

In addition to financial measures of performance, some researchers have considered softer measures, such as 'innovativeness', 'ethical standing', 'environmental responsibility', 'employment prospects', 'employee conditions', 'industrial relations' and 'legal standing' (Saul 1983, Carroll 1979 and Goldsmith and Clutterbuck 1984). Although these issues are difficult to gauge, some of the most seminal studies have incorporated at least some of them, by seeking the advice of knowledgeable individuals in the business community (Carter and Williams 1957 and Peters and Waterman 1982).

The research objectives necessitated a research design which would be flexible enough to explain strategic and tactical marketing behaviour, yet rigorous enough to allow measurement and explanation of observed behaviour. This suggests both qualitative and quantitative designs. Accordingly, a two-staged survey was designed. The first stage involved semi-structured interviews with a cross-section of opinion leaders, including members of the CBI's Marketing Committee, directors of various EDCs, the director general of the Institute of Marketing, and management writers. The purpose of this stage was to solicit views and opinions about good marketing practice, factors discriminating between success and failure in business, differences between high- and low-growth industries and to pilot the operationalisation of certain variables for the second stage. The second stage involved structured interviews with managing directors in 43 above-average and 43 below-average companies, which is explained later. (One company's performance figures are unavailable).

The Pilot Survey: Survey of Opinion Leaders

Sample

Members of the CBI's Marketing Committee involved in manufacturing industry were contacted, along with several leading management writers and publishers. Seven opinion leaders agreed to be interviewed: five were members of the Marketing Committee and two were management writers. These interviews, together with preliminary desk research, facilitated the identification of the industry sectors of interest. A number of key informants for each industry — from the relevant EDCs and Trade Associations — were contacted. This resulted in a further seven pilot interviews (see Table 5.1).

Schedule Design and Interview Process

As this stage was exploratory a loosely-structured schedule was designed to promote discussion of the major area of interest. The conversations were tape-recorded to ease the flow of discussion and achieve greater accuracy in reporting data. Full transcriptions of the tape recordings were taken, and the findings were applied to increase the content validity of the questionnaire used at the next stage in the research.

The Interview Survey:

Sample Selection

The sample frame was selected carefully, to reflect a range of industry categories and company sizes. Several previous research

Table 5.1 Sample of Opinion Leaders

CBI marketing committee members	5
Management writers	2
Representatives of trade associations	3
Key informants from economic development councils	4
Total	14

studies have concentrated on 'sunrise' or 'growth' industries. As previously explained, such an approach often means that it is difficult to say whether companies are successful because of their operations or in spite of them. The current study was therefore based on both 'sunrise' (high-growth) and 'sunset' (low-growth) industries.

Industry growth rates were calculated from ICC's *Industrial Performance Analysis 1985/86*. The analysis details 25 'industries' and 134 'industry sectors'. A number of measures were used to calculate performance. Three criteria were used in the selection of low and high growth industries, because they are widely understood and usually available in company reports and other published sources of company performance. They are:

(i)   Sales growth   (1981−4)
(ii) Average profit margin   (1981−4)
(iii) Average return on capital employed   (1981−4)

The composite sales growth for British Industry was 11 per cent, the average profit margin was 4.65 per cent, and the average return on capital employed was 13.3 per cent. The chosen sectors of manufacturing industry which were above average on all three measures were: electronics, medical equipment, and pharmaceuticals; the sectors which were below average on all three were: agricultural equipment, paper and board manufacturers, and sports and toys manufacturers. Within these six industry sectors a number of above- and below-average firms were included in the sample frame. A company was deemed 'above average' when both its composite sales growth and average profit margin, from 1981 to 1984, were above the particular industry's average.

Within the sectors, the selection was made so that small (below 200 employees), medium-sized (200−499) and large (over 500 employees) companies were represented. The selection of companies in the sample was not statistically random since the sales growth and average profit had to be calculated as they were the basis of stratification and selection. Companies were only selected if both composite sales growth and average profits were above or below the average for the industry. Companies with above-average sales growth and below-average profits are not, therefore, represented. Similarly, companies with below-average sales growth and above-average profits are not represented. Originally, it was intended to draw a sample of 200 companies so that, with an anticipated response rate of 50 per cent, 100 companies could be interviewed. However, this was impossible for, given the available sources of company data used (*Kompass: MacMillan's Top 50,000*), not enough companies could be found to fit into the size and performance categories. The final request sample is given in Table 5.2. It includes a seventh industry which was above-average in performance: food processing.

Research Instrument

A detailed and lengthy questionnaire was drawn up based on the findings of the literature review and semi-structured interviews. The schedule, which was fully structured, was divided into three parts: section A was concerned with organisation and strategy, section B investigated various aspects of business practice, while section C was a short self-completion section which examined the attitudes of managers to marketing. A selection of question types, closed and open, were included in the questionnaire to collect the desired data and maintain the respondent's interest. The questionnaire was piloted on five company directors: two managing directors, two marketing directors and one company secretary. It was also critically examined by experienced research staff in the Marketing Department, University of Strathclyde. After piloting, the questionnaire was re-worked and reproduced in the final form.

Given the geographical spread of companies in the sample frame, it was decided that the most economical method of carrying out the interviews was to assign the work to a market research agency. The agency carried out the fieldwork, although the analysis was carried out by the authors.

Sample Demographics

The composition of the final sample, broken down by industry and company size, is given in Table 5.2. In order to locate possible sources of response bias, the x^2 statistic was calculated for variations among the stratum response sample sizes (n) in Table 5.2. This statistic ($x^2 = 14.8\ df = 12\ p = 0.24$) indicated that there

Table 5.2 Sample Information

	Electronics manufacturers	Medical equipment	Agricultural equipment	Paper & board	Pharmaceuticals	Sports & toys	Food processing	Total
Small	$m = 11$	$m = 15$	$m = 11$	$m = 15$	$m = 17$	$m = 18$	$m = 5$	$m = 92$
	$n = 5$	$n = 6$	$n = 9$	$n = 8$	$n = 5$	$n = 3$	$n = 4$	$n = 40$
	$r = 0.45$	$r = 0.81$	$r = 0.81$	$r = 0.30$	$r = 0.16$	$r = 0.16$	$r = 0.80$	$m = 0.43$
Medium	$m = 15$	$m = 3$	$m = 6$	$m = 13$	$m = 6$	$m = 7$	$m = 1$	$m = 51$
	$n = 5$	$n = 3$	$n = 3$	$n = 10$	$n = 0$	$n = 5$	$n = 0$	$n = 26$
	$r = 1.0$	$r = 1.0$	$r = 0.5$	$r = 0.77$	$r = 0$	$r = 0.71$	$r = 0$	$m = 0.63$
Large	$m = 11$	$m = 9$	$m = 4$	$m = 10$	$m = 15$	$m = 6$	$m = 4$	$m = 59$
	$n = 2$	$n = 4$	$n = 3$	$n = 3$	$n = 2$	$n = 1$	$n = 3$	$n = 18$
	$r = 0.18$	$r = 0.44$	$r = 0.75$	$r = 0.3$	$r = 0.13$	$r = 0.17$	$r = 0.75$	$r = 0.30$
Total	$m_1 = 37$	$m_1 = 27$	$m_1 = 21$	$m_1 = 38$	$m_1 = 38$	$m_1 = 31$	$m_1 = 10$	$m = 202$
	$n_1 = 12$	$n_1 = 13$	$n_1 = 15$	$n_1 = 21$	$n_1 = 7$	$n_1 = 9$	$n_1 = 7$	$n = 84^*$
	$r = 0.44$	$r = 0.48$	$r = 0.71$	$r = 0.55$	$r = 0.18$	$r = 0.29$	$r = 0.70$	$r = 0.45$

Notes: m = request sample size; n = actual sample size; r = response rate.
* size categories unavailable due to non-response.

Table 5.3 Successful and Less Successful Companies in Each Industry

Industry	Number of companies (%)		
	Successful	*Less successful*	*Total*
Electronics	6 (50%)	6 (50%)	12
Medical equipment	3 (23%)	10 (77%)	13
Agricultural equipment	9 (60%)	6 (40%)	15
Paper and board	12 (51%)	9 (43%)	21
Pharmaceuticals	5 (63%)	3 (37%)	8
Sports and toys	5 (50%)	5 (50%)	10
Food products	3 (43%)	4 (57%)	7
	43	43	86

Note: sample size = 86; 1 company substituted from original list, and cannot be categorised accurately.

was no overall response bias due to company size or industry category.

Table 5.3 shows the final sample broken down by industry and success grouping. Again, the x^2 statistic indicated that no one industry contained a significantly higher number of successful companies ($x^2 = 6.0\ df = 6\ p = 0.42$). The final sample size of 87 companies represented 45 per cent of the possible 192 firms, which compared well with similar studies of this nature (Hansen 1980, Dubinsky and Ingram 1982).

Table 5.4 shows the breakdown of successful and less successful companies by the performance rate of the industry. As can be seen, of the 40 companies in the sunrise industries, 17 (43 per cent) were above average. Of the 40 companies in the sunset industries, 26 (56 per cent) were above average.

Table 5.4 Company References in the 'Sunrise' (Above-average) and 'Sunset' (Below-average) Industry

Company	Industry		
	Sunrise	*Sunset*	*Total*
Above-average	17 (43%)	26 (56%)	43
Below-average	23 (58%)	30 (44%)	43

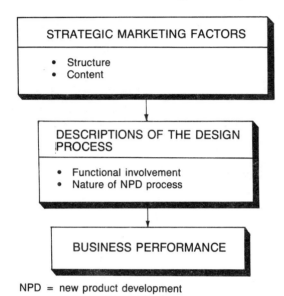

NPD = new product development

Figure 5.2 A Conceptual Framework for Profit by Design

5.2 Profit by Design

Profit by Design has a narrower focus than Project MACS, focusing on design factors that might help to explain superior commercial performance. This said, an underlying assumption of the study was that the design of market-led, successful products depends, in part, on top management's commitment to, and support of, both design and marketing functions in the company. There was, therefore, a strategic focus on Profit by Design. The framework upon which the research was based is shown in Figure 5.2.

At least three major difficulties face any research into concepts like marketing, design, competitiveness and business success or failure. First, the problem is one of definition. None of these states or activities is absolute — they reside somewhere on a continuum between zero and infinity. Accordingly, all findings must be couched in comparative — more than/less than — terms. A further difficulty is that of measurement and it stems, at least in part, from the problem of definition. Apart from a few concrete measures such as sales volume, return on investment, etc., one has to resort to surrogate measures in order to assess an organisation's *commitment* to an activity, like market research or design, or an attitude or policy, such as a marketing/design orientation. Further, surrogate measures will usually be found to vary in a material way depending upon the size and nature of organisation being studied. The final difficulty is that of bias. Marketing, design, communication, etc. are clearly 'a good thing'. It would be surprising, therefore, if respondents did not tend to overstate their beliefs or commitments if questioned directly on such issues.

In undertaking a survey into design practice in engineering and textile companies in Scotland, the study attempted to address these difficulties as follows. First, in similar fashion to Project MACS, success/failure was defined in terms of the performance of the respondent companies compared with the average performance for the industry/market in which they competed. Second, we confined the study to companies of approximately the same size (less than 250 employees). Third, we couched the whole survey in terms of a company activity in which all functions may be expected to participate to some degree — new product development. Finally, we defined design in terms of both *engineering* ('the use of scientific principles, technical information and imagination in the definition of a mechanical structure, machine or system to perform pre-specified functions with the maximum economy and efficiency', Roy and Bruce (1984)) and *aesthetics* ('another term for industrial or human factors design which takes into account the style, appearance and ergonomics of a product') so that respondents could distinguish these as separate functions alongside R & D, manufacturing, marketing, etc.

Sample

The researchers compiled the sampling frame after consultation with the Design Council (Scotland) and the Scottish Development Agency (Table 5.5).

The engineering and textiles sectors were selected specifically to meet the following criteria:

1. Increasing import penetration: in December 1978 the Central Statistical Office reported import penetration in tex-

Table 5.5 Sampling Frame

| | Company Size (Employees) | | |
Industry	1–100	101–250	250+
Engineering	35	20	5
Textiles	10	7	3

Note: Total number of companies = 80

tiles as 25 per cent of the total UK market; in June 1984 it stood at 35 per cent. Similarly in engineering, import penetration rose from 21 per cent in December 1978 to 23 per cent in June 1984.

2. Decreasing export sales: the Central Statistical Office reported that textile exports had decreased from 20 per cent of the total UK market in December 1978 to 19 per cent in June 1984. In the engineering sector, exports decreased from 35 per cent in December 1978 to 31 per cent in June 1984.

3. Both industries are significant to the Scottish economy in terms of numbers employed.

4. There are examples of successful companies in the industries.

5. There are small and medium-sized companies in the industries.

6. There are examples of companies exporting.

The companies in the sample were drawn from the manufacturing classifications of the Scottish Council for Development and Industry publication which stratifies manufacturing companies by industry, employment size and exports.

Research Instrument

A questionnaire was drawn up from an extensive literature review and discussions with the Design Council (Scotland). The questionnaire consisted of two parts: part A was a short self-completion section on company financial and background information; part

B was a fully structured questionnaire to be administered to managing directors during a prearranged interview. Prearranged personal interviews were considered by the researchers to be the optimum method of guaranteeing that the information would be supplied by managing directors. The questionnaire comprised multiple-choice questions and open-ended questions.

Two specific areas were covered by the questionnaire: strategic business issues and new product development. The research instrument was specifically developed around the topic of new product development rather than product design in order to attempt to minimise respondent bias. It was felt that bias might occur for two reasons: because design is an emotive concept and thus open to varied interpretation; or due to the well-established fact that respondents like to 'help' interviewers by giving answers they think the research wants.

The questionnaire was extensively piloted on five company directors from various backgrounds — managing director, marketing director, and company secretary. The questionnaire was also subjected to the scrutiny of the experienced research staff of the Department of Marketing, Strathclyde University.

Sample Demographics

The composition of the sample reflects the original preferences of the sponsors, in terms of the industries represented and numbers employed. Table 5.6 depicts the sample broken down by size and industry.

Table 5.6 Company Size by Industry

| Industry | Company Size (Number of Employees) | | | |
	Fewer than 100	101–250	More than 250	Total
Engineering	23 (55%)	15 (36%)	4 (9%)	42 (100%)
Textiles	9 (47%)	7 (37%)	3 (16%)	19 (100%)
Total	32 (52%)	22 (36%)	7 (12%)	61 (100%)

The majority of sample companies are located in the engineering sector (41 companies, 62 per cent) and, in terms of company size, have fewer than 100 employees (32 companies, 52 per cent).

One aim of this research was to identify design factors which contribute to company success. A number of measures of success were considered and these are listed in the Appendix to this chapter. Two measures were selected as they met the criteria specified earlier: average sales growth and average profit growth. Average profit growth was excluded from the analysis for two reasons. First, the majority of companies in the sample were not willing to disclose this information to the researchers, nor were they obliged to divulge the information to Companies' House in Edinburgh. Second, profit as a measure of success is open to manipulation by different accounting practices. Average sales growth was calculated for the sample companies over a period of four years, from the year ending 1982 to the year ending 1985. Table 5.7 details the calculations.

Profit by Design was also based on high- and low-growth industries. The engineering industry, with composite sales

Table 5.7 Example of Average Sales Growth

	1982	1983	1984	1985
Sales (£000's)	1,000	1,400	1,800	2,200
Sales Growth		40%	29%	22%

$$\frac{\text{Average Sales Growth}}{\text{Time}} = \frac{40 + 29 + 22}{3} = 30\%$$

Table 5.8

	Industry	
Company	Sunrise	Sunset
Above-average	15 (79%)	20 (48%)
Below-average	4 (21%)	22 (52%)

growth of 6 per cent and average profits of 2.9 per cent, represented a low-growth industry, while the textile sector represented an above-average manufacturing sector, with a composite growth figure of 25 per cent and average profits of 5 per cent.

From a request sample of 140 companies, 61 took part in the survey — a response rate of 44 per cent. Of the 42 companies in the engineering (sunset) industry, 20 (48 per cent) were above average. In the textile industry, however, 15 (79 per cent) of the 19 companies were above-average (Table 5.8). Having described the two surveys, the next chapter reports their major findings.

Appendix: Performance Measures (Financial)

	Authors
(A) SALES BASED	
1. Gross sales	Fredrickson (1984, June, Sept); Thune and House (1970); Karger and Malik (1975); Saul (1983)
2. Sales turnover	Channon (1979); *Scottish Business Insider* (1985)
3. Sales revenue	Boyd (1984)
4. Return on sales	Peters and Waterman (1982)
5. Sales growth	McKinsey (1983); Roy (1987)
(B) PROFIT BASED	
1. Return on investment	Cooper (1984); Woo and Cooper (1982); Snow and Hrebiniak (1980); Boyd (1984)
2. Profitability	Allen and Panian (1982); Chaganti and Chaganti (1983); Weiner and Mahoney (1981)
3. Profit margin	Hooley *et al.* (1984); Weiner and Mahoney (1981); Roy (1987)
4. Profit before tax	*Scottish Business Insider* (1985)
5. Profit after tax	Schendel, Patton and Riggs (1976)
6. Profit growth	McKinsey (1983)

(C)   CAPITAL BASED

    1. Return on   Thune and House (1970); Channon (1979);
       capital employed   Karger and Malik (1975); Peters and
       (before/after tax)   Waterman (1982)

(D)   EQUITY BASED

    1. Return on equity   Peters and Waterman (1982); Thune and
                        House (1970); McKinsey (1983); Allen
                        and Panian (1982)

    2. Equity Growth   Peters and Waterman (1982)

    3. Share (stock)   Thune and House (1970); Weiner and
       prices   Mahoney (1981); Karger and Malik
                        (1975); Saul (1983)

    4. Earnings per   Thune and House (1970); Channon
       share   (1979); Karger and Malik (1975)

    5. Sales per share   Karger and Malik (1975)

    6. Cash flow per   Karger and Malik (1975)
       share

    7. Book value per   Karger and Malik (1975)
       share

    8. Capital spending   Karger and Malik (1975)
       per share

    9. Percentage of   Karger and Malik (1975)
       dividends to
       income

    10. Average price/   Karger and Malik (1975)
        earnings ratio

(E)   ASSETS BASED

    1. Compound   Peters and Waterman (1982); McKinsey
       asset growth   (1983)

    2. Return on assets   Fredrickson (1984)

    3. Growth rate in   Channon (1979)
       assets per share

    4. Growth rate in   Channon (1979)
       group net assets

    5. Ratio of profits   Chaganti and Chaganti (1983)
       to total assets
       employed

6. Rate earned on net worth	Karger and Malik (1975)

(F) MISCELLANEOUS

1. Market capitalisation	*Scottish Business Insider* (1985)
2. Average ratio of market value to book value	Peters and Waterman (1982)
3. Increase in total market value	McKinsey (1983)
4. Return on resources	Saul (1983)

References

Allen, N.P. and Panian, S.K. (1982) 'Power, performance and succession in the large corporation', *Administrative Science Quarterly*, vol. 27, pp. 538–47.

Argenti, J. (1978) *Systematic Corporate Planning*, Van Nostrand Reinhold (UK).

Bell, M. (1979) *Marketing: Concepts and Strategy*, (3rd edn), Houghton Mifflin.

Boyd, D.P. (1984) 'Type A behaviour, financial performance and organisational growth in small business firms', *Journal of Occupational Psychology*, vol. 57, pp. 137–40.

Bradley, F. (1986) 'Key factors influencing international competitiveness', Symposium on International Marketing Proceedings, *Journal of Irish Business and Administrative Research*, vol. 7, no. 2, Winter.

Carroll, A.B. (1979) 'A three dimensional conceptual model of corporate performance', *Academy of Management Review*, vol. 4, no. 4, October.

Carter, C.F. and Williams, B.R. (1957) *Industry and Technical Progress*, Oxford University Press.

Chaganti, R. and Chaganti, R. (1983) 'A profile of profitable and not so profitable small businesses', *Journal of Small Business Management*, July.

Channon, D. (1979) 'Leadership and corporate performance in the service industries', *Journal of Management Studies*, vol. 16, no. 2, May.

Cooper, R.G. (1984) 'The strategy performance link in product innovation', *R and D Management*, vol. 14, issue 4.

Dubinsky, A.J. and Ingram, J.N. (1982) 'A factor-analytic study of criteria examined in the first-time sales manager promotion process', Proceedings of the 1982 Conference of the American Marketing Association.

Dunn, M.G., Norburn, D. and Birley, S. (1985) 'Corporate culture: a positive correlate with marketing effectiveness', *International Journal of Advertising*, vol. 4, pp. 65–73.

Ferguson, C.R. and Dickenson, R. (1981) 'Critical success factors for directors in the eighties', *Business Horizons*, May/June.

Frazier, G.L. and Howell, R.D. (1983) 'Business definitions and performance', *Journal of Marketing*, vol. 47, Spring.

Fredrickson, J.W. (1984) 'The comprehensiveness of strategic decision processes: extension, observation and future direction', *Academy of Management Journal*, vol. 27, no. 3.

Goldsmith, W. and Clutterbuck, D. (1984) *The Winning Streak: Britain's Top Companies Reveal Their Formulas for Success*, Weidenfeld & Nicolson.

Hansen, R. (1980) 'A self-perception interpretation of the effect of monetary and non-monetary incentives on mail survey respondent behaviour', *Journal of Marketing Research*, vol. 17, February.

Hooley, G.J., West, C.J. and Lynch, J.E. (1984) *Marketing in the UK: A Survey of Current Practices and Performance*, The Institute of Marketing.

ICC Business Performance Analysis, 1986/87 and 1987/88 editions, ICC Information Group, London.

Karger, P.W. and Malik, Z.A. (1975) 'Long range planning and organisational performance', *Long Range Planning*, December.

Kotler, P. (1980) *Marketing Management Analysis, Planning and Control*, (4th edn) Prentice-Hall.

McKinsey and Co. (1983) *The Winning Performance of the Midsized Growth Companies* American Business Conference, May, McKinsey and Co., London.

NEDO (1976) *The UK and West German Manufacturing Industry 1969–1972*, NEDO.

Peters, T.J. and Waterman, R.W. (1982) *In Search of Excellence*, Harper & Row.

Reece, J.S. and Cool, W.R. (1978) 'Measuring investment center performance', *Harvard Business Review*, May/June.

Roy, R. (1987) 'Design for business success', *Engineering*, January.

Roy, R. and Bruce, M. (1984) *Product Design, Innovation and Competition in British Manufacturing: Background, Aims and Methods*, Design Innovation Group, The Open University, September.

Saul, P. (1983) 'New ways of measuring company performance', *Rydge's*, vol. 56, September.

Scottish Business Insider (1985) vol. 2, issue 1, January.

Snow, C.C. and Hrebiniak, L.G. (1980) 'Strategy, distinctive competence, and organisational performance', *Administrative Science Quarterly*, vol. 25, June.

Thune, S.S. and House,P.S. (1970) 'Where long range planning pays off', *Business Horizons*, August.

Weiner, N. and Mahoney, T.A. (1981) 'A model of corporate performance as a function of environmental, organisational, and leadership influences', *Academy of Management Journal*, vol. 24, no. 3.

Woo, C.Y. and Cooper, A.C. (1982) 'The surprising case for low market share', *Harvard Business Review*, Nov./Dec.

6

The Empirical Evidence

6.1 Introduction

This chapter gives the details of the two studies described in the previous chapter. It is structured around three broad sets of marketing issues that the research projects investigated: organisational, strategic, and tactical marketing issues. Specifically, the chapter will review the similarities and differences between above-average and below-average organisations in terms of their marketing *organisation, strategy* and *tasks*. For every section of findings, a comparison was made between companies in above- and below-average industries. The former were called 'sunrise' industries, the latter 'sunset'. For more information on which industries are deemed sunrise and sunset, see Chapter 5.

Similarly, tests were carried out to check if the size of an organisation influenced its marketing organisation, strategy or tasks. As will be seen, industry and size did not have a major effect on the findings, and only where a significant effect was detected are details given in the text. The tests used for each table or figure are shown in the appendix. As was outlined in Chapter 5, the studies overlapped on several, but not all, aspects of marketing. Generally, Project MACS was the bigger study, covering more issues than Profit By Design. Their similarities and differences are shown in Table 6.1.

6.2 Organisation of Marketing

Much has been said about the need for marketing to be embraced as a total company philosophy, implying a broad, interactive role for the marketing function within the organisation. Indeed, isola-

Table 6.1 Areas of Investigation — *Project MACS* and *Profit by Design*

Area of Investigation	Project MACS	Profit by Design
Organisation		
Board composition	√	√
Board communication with lower bodies	√	
Location of marketing function		√
Strategy		
Long-term planning	√	√
Long-term objectives	√	√
Issues of relevance to strategy formulation	√	√
Strategic alternatives	√	√
Involvement in strategic decision-making	√	
Tasks		
New Product development — triggers	√	√
Involvement in the NPD process		√
Use of market research	√	
Information type and sources	√	
Marketing information systems	√	
Market segmentation	√	
Service to the customer	√	
Customer contact	√	
Sales management	√	
Distribution objectives and practices	√	
Promotional media	√	
Pricing	√	

tion of the marketing function and its lack of authority has been put forward as evidence of lack of commitment to marketing (Webster 1981, Piercy 1985 and Rothwell 1974). Both Project MACS and Profit by Design looked at the issue of the status of marketing.

First, both studies looked at which functions were given Board-level status. Table 6.2 shows the composition of the Board for the companies investigated by Project MACS and Profit by Design respectively.

Table 6.2 Composition of the Board in the Companies Under Study in Project MACS and Profit by Design

Title	Project MACS (total sample — 86) %	Profit by Design (total sample — 58) %
Managing director	87	90
Finance director	63	41
Sales director	52	45 (with Marketing)
Manufacturing director	44	43
Legal director	40	—
Chairman	37	—
Marketing director	31	9
Engineering director	28	43
Divisional director	15	—
R and D director	10	—
Technical sales director	—	10
Works manager	—	7

In both studies, no differences in the composition of the Board were found among industry categories, although a few differences were found among different sizes of firm (measured by the number of employees). In the companies surveyed by Project MACS, more large companies had marketing, finance, manufacturing and legal directors, although the differences were not statistically significant. Large companies also had more R and D directors on the Board, a difference which was significant (see Figure 6.1). As only 7 companies participating in Profit by Design employed more than 250 people, similar differences among companies of different sizes could not be detected.

However, for the two samples, variation in Board composition according to the performance of companies was the real issue of interest. There was no such variation in Profit by Design's sample. In the latter case, more above-average companies mentioned the managing director's membership of the Board, and the engineering director. The variations in Project MACS are shown in Table 6.3.

Project MACS, recognising that marketing may be included in key top-level decisions, also investigated the frequency with which successful and unsuccessful companies have marketing

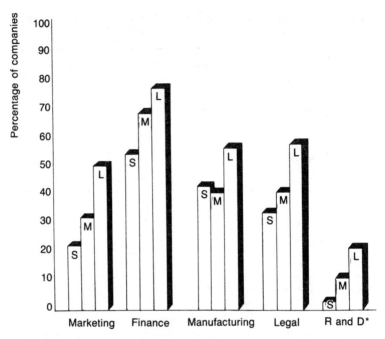

Notes: * Significant at the 10 per cent level.
        S Small (fewer than 200 employees).
        M Medium (200–499 employees).
        L Large (over 500 employees).

Figure 6.1 Differences in Board Composition by Company Size
            – Project MACS

personnel meet with the executive decision-making body. As can be seen from Table 6.4, more successful companies have these meetings more often. Profit by Design, whose sample featured a majority of small companies (employing fewer than 250 people) looked at the extent to which a marketing *function* existed in companies, and where such a function might be located. This proved to be an important distinction since, in small companies, *organisational commitment* to marketing need not be synonymous with the existence of a marketing *department* (Walsh and Roy 1983 and Piercy 1985). For the purposes of the study, if no one in the company is *responsible* for marketing, then no marketing *function* exists. The findings are depicted in Figure 6.2. These findings show that 92 per cent of the sample had a marketing function:

Table 6.3 Differences in Board Composition between Above- and Below-average Companies — Project MACS

Title	Above-average companies (total sample 43)	Below-average companies (total sample 43)	Above-average variation from below-average†
Managing director	93%	81%	+ 15%*
Chairman	31%	43%	− 28%
Engineering director	36%	17%	+111%*
Manufacturing director	38%	49%	− 23%

Notes: * Significant at the 10 per cent level.
      † The variation is calculated by dividing the above-average percentage by that of the below-average percentage. Where above-average companies adopt a particular answer *more* often, a positive variation is shown. Where they adopt it *less* often, a negative variation is shown.

Table 6.4 The Frequency of Executive Marketing Meetings in Successful and Unsuccessful Companies

	Total sample (total sample 86)	Successful firms (total sample 43)	Unsuccessful firms (total sample 43)	Successful firms' variation from unsuccessful firms'
Infrequently	7%	0%	14%	− ∞
Sometimes	22%	25%	19%	+32%*
Often	70%	75%	67%	+12%

Note: * Significant at the 5 per cent level.

55 per cent were located within a marketing or sales department, 12 per cent were in general administration and 8 per cent looked to a parent company for advice. The companies that relied on the parent company for advice belonged exclusively to the average and negative sales growth groups. All the companies which had no marketing function had either average or negative sales growth. By contrast, *all* the high growth companies had a marketing function located in either a marketing or sales department.

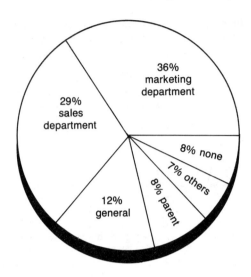

Figure 6.2 Location of the Marketing Function

Reprise

To conclude this section on the organisation and integration of
marketing in business, the findings presented show that the
existence of departments and Board titles is as much a function
of the size of companies as it is of their commitment to a particular function or philosophy. This said, more subtle ways of
assessing a company's commitment — such as whether there is
any marketing carried out, or whether personnel responsible for
marketing meet frequently with the executive committee — do
show differences between more and less successful firms (Table
6.5).

6.3   Strategic Marketing Planning

Considerable anecdotal evidence supports the contention that success in any given area of business activity is enhanced if commitment to that activity is enshrined in the company's strategic plan.
(Walsh and Roy 1983, Hooley and Lynch 1985 and Saunders and
Wong 1985). Moreover, there has been much debate over the

Table 6.5 Organisation and Integration of Marketing in Above-average
and Below-average Companies

Above-average Companies

• Marketing personnel meet more frequently with the top-level
  decision-making committee.

• Marketing responsibility is defined within a sales and/or
  marketing department.

Below-average Companies

• Marketing personnel meet less frequently with the top-level
  decision-making committee.

• Marketing responsibility is left to the parent company.

• Marketing responsibility is isolated in general-purpose, support
  functions.

apparent subjugation of a long-term approach to business by
short-term profit maximisation in British companies, which is said
to account for their comparative lack of success (Webster 1981,
Hayes and Abernathy 1980 and King 1985). The research findings
of both MACS and Profit by Design serve to emphasise the
association between success and a long-term approach to business
planning, irrespective of industry or company size (see Table 6.6).

Table 6.6 Strategic Planning* in Successful and Less Successful
Companies

		Does your company engage in strategic planning?		
Study	Total sample	Above-average companies	Below-average companies	Variation
MACS 'Yes'	(86)	(43) 98%	(43) 78%	+26%#
Profit by Design 'Yes'	(61)	(35) 86%	(26) 68%	+26% ᴬ

Notes: *   Defined as planning beyond the next 18 months.
     #   Significant at the 5 per cent level.
     ᴬ   Significant at the 10 per cent level.

MOUNT PLEASANT LIBRARY
TEL. 051 207 3581 Ext. 3701

Table 6.7 The Time Horizon of Strategic Plans in Above- and Below-
average Companies — Project MACS

Number of years	Sample size (86)	Above-average companies (43)	Below-average companies (43)	Variation
<2		7%	31%	−87%
3–4		38%	27%	+38%
>5		57%	42%	+36%

Note: Significant at the 5 per cent level.

In a similar way, project MACS confirmed that the length of time covered by strategic plans is also associated with company success (Table 6.7). Although it might be reasonable to assume that larger firms have more resources to devote to an activity like strategic planning, or that the bigger companies might tend to plan for longer periods of time, no such relationship was found. Similarly, no great differences could be found in strategic horizon between sunrise and sunset industries.

It is part of conventional wisdom that objectives, even long-term ones, have to be quantified if they are to be used meaningfully in organisations. Indeed, the idea that any strategy will only be successful if it can be effectively implemented, suggests that companies will need benchmarks against which to measure implementation.

In both MACS and Profit by Design, more successful companies *quantified* their long-term objectives, giving themselves tangible standards against which to judge their performance (see Table 6.8). In order to take a closer look at the elements of strategic planning, both studies investigated respondents' opinions regarding the relevance of a number of issues to their strategic planning.

The sample companies were asked to rate the relevance of each strategic planning issue on a five-point scale, where 5 signified 'extremely relevant' and 1 signified 'not at all relevant'. In both, the average scores of above- and below-average companies were tested (using a t-test) to see if there were any statistically significant differences. Figure 6.3 shows the average scores for each group of companies in Project MACS. As can be seen from the

Table 6.8 Long-term Objectives in Above- and Below-average Companies

		Are long-term objectives quantified?		
Study	Total sample	Above-average companies	Below-average companies	Variation
MACS	(86)	(43)	(43)	
'Yes'		87%	71%	+23%
PROFIT BY DESIGN	(61)	(35)	(26)	
'Yes'		87%	69%	+26%

Note: Significant at the 10 per cent level.

figure, the successful and unsuccessful companies have similar views on the relevance of most of the strategic issues. This was similar in the Profit by Design companies (Figure 6.4).

Both figures show that the more successful companies in MACS found forecasts of market share to be more relevant, while those in Profit by Design attached more importance to cash flow considerations and *continuous* process and product improvement. Also interesting is the fact that unsuccessful MACS companies felt that new product development and export volume were more relevant than did the more successful companies. This might well be indicative of the companies' recognition of the need to pursue these activities, given the considerable amount of encouragement to do so found in the business pages of the press. (It also highlights the difficulty of using *past* philosophy as an indicator of *future* performance).

By far the most striking feature of Figures 6.3 and 6.4 is that there are relatively *few* differences between both groups of above- and below-average companies. This lends considerable weight to criticisms of research that looks at the operating methods of successful companies *only* as indicators of how best to run a business. When research controls the effect of industry environment or company size, and compares the operating methods of successful companies with those of less successful companies, the usual battery of strategic issues no longer distinguishes between the two.

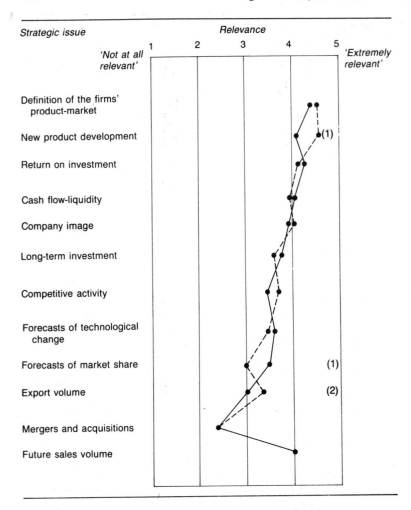

——— Successful companies
– – – – Unsuccessful companies

Notes: (1) Significant difference at the 5 per cent level (sum of both tails).
        (2) Significant difference at the 10 per cent level (sum of both tails).

Figure 6.3   Strategic Issues in Above- and Below-average Companies
            – Project MACS

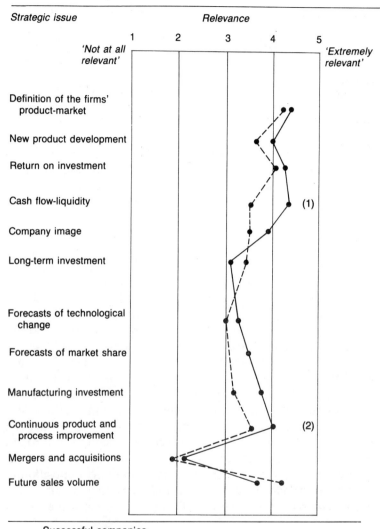

Strategic issue | Relevance

1 2 3 4 5
'Not at all relevant'   'Extremely relevant'

Definition of the firms' product-market

New product development

Return on investment

Cash flow-liquidity   (1)

Company image

Long-term investment

Forecasts of technological change

Forecasts of market share

Manufacturing investment

Continuous product and process improvement   (2)

Mergers and acquisitions

Future sales volume

———— Successful companies
– – – – Unsuccessful companies

Notes: (1) Significant difference at the 5 per cent level (sum of both tails).
(2) Significant difference at the 10 per cent level (sum of both tails).

Figure 6.4 Strategic Issues in Above- and Below-average Companies
– Profit by Design

As many business people already know, there is no simple formula for success. Even if there were, it would soon be adopted by less successful firms and would itself disappear as a distinguishing feature!

As well as looking at what managers consider relevant to their strategic planning process, both MACS and Profit by Design strategies studied the importance of five basic strategies of business, based on Ansoff's (1968) growth-vector matrix (see Table 6.9). (A fifth strategy, *developing products with a higher added value*, was included as it was of interest to the sponsors of one of the studies; it can be viewed as a way of pursuing both product and market development.) Project MACS merely examined whether or not each strategy was pursued by the companies in the sample. As Table 6.10 shows, all the strategies are well used. Profit by Design sought to gauge the perceived importance of each strategy and asked respondents to rate each one on a five-point scale, where 1 signified 'not at all important' and 5 signified 'extremely important'. Table 6.11 shows the strategies ordered by their average rating; diversification (developing new products for new markets) was not included in this study.

Figure 6.5 shows the average scores for both successful and less successful companies in Profit by Design, while Figure 6.6 shows the usage of each strategy by MACS's above- and below-average companies. In general, the successful companies in Profit by Design thought *every* strategy more important than did less successful ones, although market penetration and market development proved to be significantly more important. This means that the route to achieving strategic objectives is seen to be through high volume sales of products in current and future markets. This is often highlighted as a strategy that is in direct opposition to the British formula of cutting costs and improving margins. Successful companies in Project MACS tended to seek achievement

Table 6.9 Ansoff's Growth–Vector Matrix

Mission ⟍ Product	Present	New
Present	Market penetration	Product development
New	Market development	Diversification

Table 6.10 The Use of Business Strategies — Project MACS

Strategy	Percentage of companies using
Market penetration	92
Product development	94
Market development	77
Diversification	70
Developing products with a higher added value	70

Table 6.11 The Importance of Business Strategy — Profit by Design

Strategy	Average score of importance (on a scale of 1 to 5)
Market penetration	4.1
Product development	3.8
Market development	3.8
Developing products with a higher added value	2.1

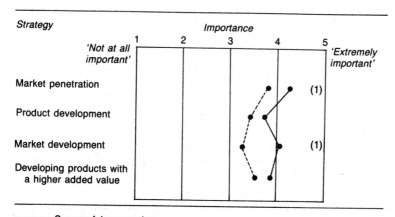

———— Successful companies
— — —+— Unsuccessful companies

Note: (1) Significant at the 10 per cent level (sum of both tails).

Figure 6.5 Business Strategies in Above- and Below-average Companies — Profit by Design

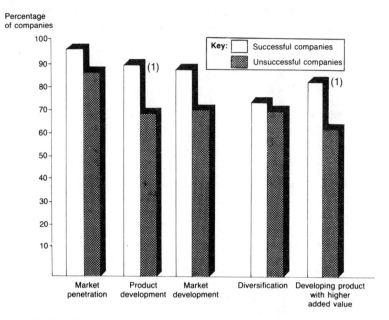

Note: (1) Significant at the 5 per cent level.

Figure 6.6 Business Strategies in Above- and Below-average
                Companies — Project MACS

of strategic objectives through product development, specifically
on development of products with higher added value.

Reprise

In conclusion to this section on strategic marketing, these studies
have pinpointed a few strategic factors which do distinguish between above- and below-average companies. For instance, taking a long-term approach to business seems to be carried out to
a greater extent in above-average companies. Indeed, commitment to specific, quantified and measurable long-term objectives
is more apparent in successful firms. Additionally, basing strategic
plans on forecasts of movements in the market-place, giving
backup to *constant* product and process improvement, but not
sacrificing company liquidity to do so are the issues relevant to

Table 6.12 Strategic Marketing in Above-average Companies

Above-average Companies

- do more strategic planning;
- have plans covering *longer* time horizons;
- quantify strategic objectives more frequently;
- are more aware of the strategic relevance of forecasts of market share;
- are more aware of the strategic importance of liquidity;
- are more aware of the strategic importance of continuous product and process development;
- follow strategies of *market penetration* (building sales of current products in current markets), *market development* (building sales of current products in new markets) and *product development* (introducing new products with higher added value into current markets).

---

strategic planning that distinguish between above- and below-average performers. Similarly, the strategies of increasing sales volume, extending volume into new market segments, and developing new products with a higher added value to serve existing markets all distinguish successful firms from less successful ones. These are summarised in Table 6.12.

Despite these differences between the successful and less successful companies in both studies, what is clear is that many of the so-called 'keys' to success — for example defining the scope of business carefully, forecasting technological change or looking after the company's image — are not exclusive to above-average performers only. Indeed, even where our findings show a *statistically* significant difference between what successful and less successful companies do, often a good many less successful companies *are* carrying out that very task. Take, for example, the issue of long-term planning. Although this factor 'separates' the two groups of companies in both studies, in MACS 78 per cent of below-average companies carried out this function, while 68 per cent of below-average Profit by Design companies also engaged in long-term planning. Little wonder then, that managers, faced with previous advice to develop long-term plans, might be disenchanted when results are not as expected. In many of today's competitive environments, the so-called 'keys' to success are merely signs that competitors are in a position to compete!

6.4 Market Tasks

A number of tactical marketing issues — tasks — were investigated by the studies, ranging from new product development to customer service and pricing techniques. The results are presented and discussed below. Both MACS and Profit by Design looked at facets of new product development, but only MACS, as the bigger study, focused on other elements of the marketing mix developed in Chapter 5.

New Product Development

There is a considerable amount of important research in the field of New Product Development (NPD) which has highlighted factors explaining successful NPD. Many of these factors stress the need for companies to take a proactive, but market-relevant approach to developing new products. Taking this research as a lead, both MACS and Profit by Design focused on the origin of the decision to develop new products to see if any 'triggers' were specific to high or low performers. The list of triggers of NPD was derived from previous research in the case of MACS and from preliminary interview in Profit by Design. Respondents were asked to indicate how important each trigger was in prompting their decisions to develop new products. A five-point scale was used, where 1 signified 'not at all important' and 5 signified 'extremely important'. Figures 6.7 and 6.8 show the importance given each trigger by successful and unsuccessful companies in MACS and Profit by Design.

In MACS, the remedial action taken to correct 'loss of existing market share' was significantly more important to less successful companies, while in Profit by Design, successful companies found that style and aesthetic factors triggering NPD were more important.

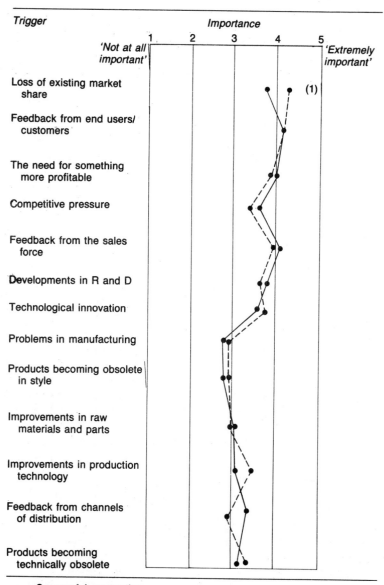

Trigger — Importance

1 'Not at all important' ... 5 'Extremely important'

- Loss of existing market share (1)
- Feedback from end users/ customers
- The need for something more profitable
- Competitive pressure
- Feedback from the sales force
- Developments in R and D
- Technological innovation
- Problems in manufacturing
- Products becoming obsolete in style
- Improvements in raw materials and parts
- Improvements in production technology
- Feedback from channels of distribution
- Products becoming technically obsolete

—— Successful companies.
––– Unsuccessful companies.
Note: (1) Significant at the 5 per cent level (sum of both tails).

Figure 6.7 NPD Triggers in Above- and Below-average Companies –
Project MACS

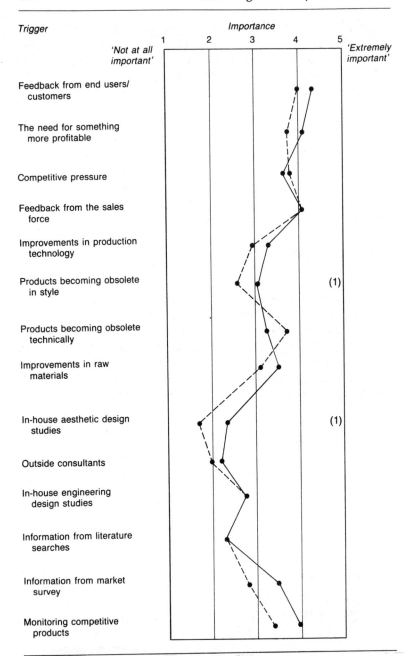

Trigger

Importance

'Not at all important'   'Extremely important'

Feedback from end users/ customers

The need for something more profitable

Competitive pressure

Feedback from the sales force

Improvements in production technology

Products becoming obsolete in style

Products becoming obsolete technically

Improvements in raw materials

In-house aesthetic design studies

Outside consultants

In-house engineering design studies

Information from literature searches

Information from market survey

Monitoring competitive products

——— Successful companies.
---- Unsuccessful companies.

Note: (1) Significant at the 5 per cent level (sum of both tails).

Figure 6.8 NPD Triggers in Above- and Below-average Companies – Profit by Design

Differences between industries were not very great, although as might be expected, the sunrise-industry companies rated 'competitive pressure' and 'technological innovation' more highly than did sunset-industry companies. Sunset-industry companies, however, thought feedback from distribution channels to be of greater importance than sunrise-industry companies.

Profit by Design also investigated the way in which the task of new product development was organised. Data were collected on the involvement of personnel throughout the new product development process. The process was split into five stages: opportunity → design → prototype development → prototype evaluation → introduction. Involvement was measured on a three-point scale where 3 signified 'extremely involved' and 1 signified 'not at all involved'. Tests were carried out to see if there were any differences in the involvement of different functions throughout the NPD process between above- and below-average companies. (Due to the nature of the data, non parametric tests were used.) In above-average companies, there are a variety of functions involved in the process (see Table 6.13).

Aesthetic design plays a significantly more extensive role throughout the NPD process in above-average companies: more precisely at the introduction stage there is greater aesthetic design involvement in above-average companies. These findings concur with those of previous studies, which have shown that successful new product introduction requires integration between marketing people and the rest of the NPD team, particularly the design element (Alexander 1985, Bruce 1985 and Challis 1983). When this occurs, there is a greater likelihood of market feedback and greater opportunity to modify early mistakes in light of new information on a dynamic market-place.

Market Research

Familiarity with customers' needs is the linchpin of a marketing orientation, and active market research has frequently been associated with successful new products and successful exporting. This said, many approaches to investigating whether market research is used in a company have been criticised for their tendency to count heads in market research departments or

Table 6.13 Differences in Functional Involvement in the NPD Process
Between Above- and Below-average Companies

	Mean Rank* for		
Stage in the decision and functional involvement	*Above-average companies*	*Below-average companies*	*Significance (%)*
OPPORTUNITY IDENTIFICATION			
Aesthetic design	20.5	12.5	5
DESIGN			
R and D	23.1	17.7	10
Aesthetic design	20.5	13.1	10
PROTOTYPE DEVELOPMENT			
Finance	28.7	21.3	5
Aesthetic design	20.5	13.1	5
Quality control	27.1	21.2	10
PROTOTYPE EVALUATION			
Marketing	27.2	20.3	5
INTRODUCTION			
Marketing	28.0	23.7	10
R and D	25.2	14.3	1
Engineering design	24.1	13.8	1
Aesthetic design	21.2	14.7	10

Note: * The mean rank is the average ranking of the raw scores for each
variable in the sub-sample.

estimate the size of market research budgets. These approaches
are said to focus on the 'trappings' of marketing not its substance,
since small, low-budget teams may be just as effective in gaining
an understanding of customers' needs as a large research
organisation.

With these issues in mind, Project MACS focused on whether
market research is carried out (either in-house or externally com-
missioned), what the source of information is and what kind of
internal information is collected to help the marketing information. Table 6.14 shows that more above-average companies carry
out and commission market research. No differences were
observed in the percentages of small, medium or large companies
investing in market research.

Among the sources of information (see Figure 6.9) two were
considered to be more important in above-average companies:

Table 6.14 Market Research in Above- and Below-average Companies

Research Type	Above-average companies	Below-average companies	Variation
In-house	52%	31%	+68%
External	69%	47%	+47%

Note: Significant at the 5 per cent level.

customer surveys and field experiments (such as test marketing).

It is interesting to note that those sources of information which require an active commitment in order to be tapped are more frequently used by successful companies. As more and more companies are made aware of sources of secondary data that are available relatively cheaply and without great commitment, it is only those sources which require an effort to tap that distinguish market-oriented successful companies. Salesmen's contacts and distributor surveys were more important in sunset-industry companies, confirming the traditional role played by these two.

The extent to which companies *forecast* the activities of competitors proved to be an important differentiating factor. Although only 27 (42 per cent) of the companies who were asked this question actually carried out this activity, 18 (66 per cent) of these were high performers (see Table 6.15). The fact that the awareness of competitors' future activities is sought to a significantly greater extent by above-average companies, irrespective of industry or company size, confirms Porter's (1980) contention that management *must* anticipate the strategies of their biggest competitors.

Table 6.15 Forecasting Competitor Activity in Above- and Below-average Companies

	Total sample	Above-average companies	Below-average companies	Variation
Companies who do forecast competitor activity	27	66%	34%	+94%

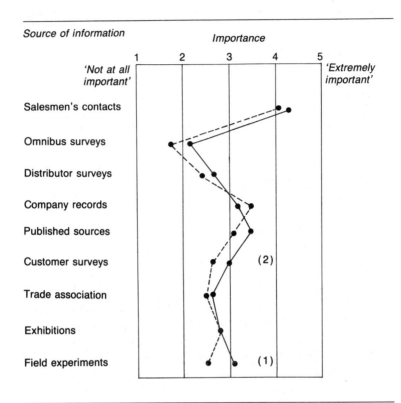

Source of information   Importance

- Successful companies.
- - - Unsuccessful companies.
Notes: (1) Significant at the 5 per cent level.
         (2) Significant at the 10 per cent level.

Figure 6.9 Information Sources in Above- and Below-average Companies

The final aspect of marketing information examined by MACS was the internal data collected by companies. Of the six types of internal information surveyed, three were collected more frequently by successful companies: stock levels, information on operational problems, and product contribution to overall sales volume (see Figure 6.10). This suggests that while a strategic focus on market share and a tactical commitment to market and com-

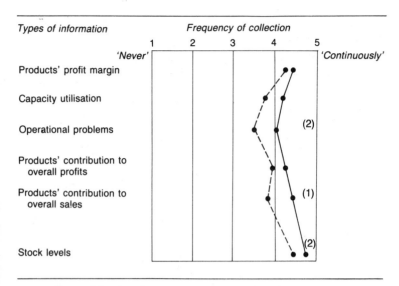

Figure 6.10 Internal Information Collected in Above- and Below-average Companies

petitor research are essential to above-average firms, they are not to the detriment of good financial control. It is important to recognise and research this as it is an aspect which 'success' research has tended to neglect. Indeed, this finding echoes that of Profit by Design, where 'liquidity' was considered more relevant to strategic planning by above-average companies. It also parallels the view expounded by Peters and Waterman (1982) that both creativity and financial control were maintained in excellent companies by their 'simultaneous loose–tight structures'.

Although no differences in the collection of internal information were found among different industries, small companies collected information about a product's contribution to overall sales and profits more frequently. Presumably, this reflects the need to ensure that scarce resources are not spread too thinly.

Market Segmentation

Conventional wisdom holds that blanket participation in all markets is less effective than a more selective approach. Project MACS sought to determine how companies segment their markets and to examine whether any differences exist between high and low performers. It is important, when speaking of marketing, to gauge the cases for segmentation and not just to relate whether or not companies segment their markets: dissecting the total business in an arbitrary way, not based on customer differences, does not indicate a strong marketing orientation. Figure 6.11 shows the way in which above- and below-average companies segment their markets.

Although none of the differences were statistically significant, as Figure 6.11 shows, above-average companies were more involved in *all* types of segmentation. In fact, when the total amount of different types are totalled for each company, the average for successful companies is 4, while for less-successful companies it is 3.4. This difference is statistically significant ($t = 1.73$, $p < 0.10$, sum of both tails). Twenty-eight per cent of companies in the sunrise industries used 'buyer demographics', while only 11 per cent of companies in the sunset industries used this. Forty per cent of sunrise-industry companies used 'benefit sought' compared to 20 per cent in the sunset industries. On the other hand, 45 per cent of sunset-industry companies used 'size of the buyer' against 25 per cent of sunrise-industry companies. These results, significant at the 10 per cent level, indicate that the industry to which a company belongs may well influence the

Table 6.16 Market Research Activities of Above-average Performers

---

Above-average companies

- More above-average companies invest in in-house and external market research.
- They are more actively involved in undertaking customer surveys and field experiments.
- They are more committed to forecasting competitive activity.
- They collect internal information more frequently.
- They are involved in more types of market segmentation.

Percentage
of companies

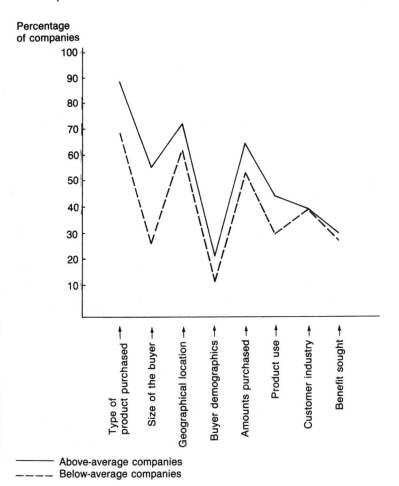

——— Above-average companies
———— Below-average companies

Figure 6.11 Segmentation in Above- and Below-average Companies

nature of its segmentation policy. Table 6.16 summarises the
market research activities of above-average companies.

Customer Care and Service

A selection of questions was used to sample the nature and extent
of the service provided by suppliers to customers. These questions related to the amount of information and advice provided,

guarantees, availability of spares, provision of credit, delivery records, and speed of after-sales service. Also investigated was the way in which the companies kept contact with their customers. This replicated directly the work of Doyle, Saunders and Wong (1985), who found that successful customer contact was achieved through calls made by executives, not merely sales people. However, only one factor differentiated between above-average and below-average companies: the supply of pre-purchase information and advice. Eighty-three per cent of above-average companies supplied these, while only 61 per cent of below-average companies did. The replication of the 'customer contact' enquiry made by Doyle, Saunders and Wong (1985) did not bring out any differences between above- and below-average companies.

Once again, it would be wrong to assume that customer care is unimportant. Rather, a majority of UK companies are now convinced of its importance, and its recognition is no longer exclusive to companies which are more competitive.

Channels of Distribution and Sales Management

Distribution is an essential element of the marketing mix. The quality of distributors, the backup and support they are given will all be reflected in the way a company's product is received in the market. One of the most distinctive features about Japanese channel management is the way in which Japanese companies do not leave their end customers entirely in the hands of unsupported dealers.

MACS looked at which type of distribution channels were used by companies and examined the objectives of and reasons for choosing their particular channels. Many companies used more than one channel of distribution, and choice seemed to be related mostly to the extant structure of the industry. For example, supplying goods 'directly to the end user' was done by 81 per cent of the sunrise-industry companies and only by 67 per cent of the sunset-industry companies. No differences between above- and below-average companies were found.

Some aspects of sales management were also examined. The importance of various qualities in sales people (experience,

technical knowledge, competitive tendency, etc.) were exa.
although there were no differences between above- and be.
average companies. Similarly, the extent to which differe.
responsibilities (increasing volume, consumer liaison, market
research) were discharged by sales people was also examined.
Again no differences between more and less successful companies
were found.

Promotion

The penultimate element of the marketing mix to be examined
by MACS was the promotional activities carried out by companies. In total, 98 per cent of the sample companies engaged
in some kind of promotion and, as can be seen from Figure 6.12,
more successful companies tended to use only a few promotional
methods much more frequently than their less successful
counterparts.

Above-average companies acted upon the need to promote their
product offering and use several low-budget types of publicity
to generate business. Only three promotional methods were used
significantly more by larger companies: television advertising,
posters and promotions designed around a specific customer, thus
dispelling the notion that promotion can only be afforded by big
companies. Sunrise-industry companies, where there is greater
need to create awareness, make significantly more use of
seminars, coupon drops, direct mail and sponsorship.

Pricing

Finally, the price of a product is always high on the list of critical
success factors. MACS looked at five basic pricing strategies to
examine whether any differences in approach could be found between successful and less successful companies. Figure 6.13 lists
the methods, and shows to what extent each method is used by
the two groups of companies. Pricing at the same level as the competition, a rather reactive strategy, is employed to a greater extent
by less successful companies.

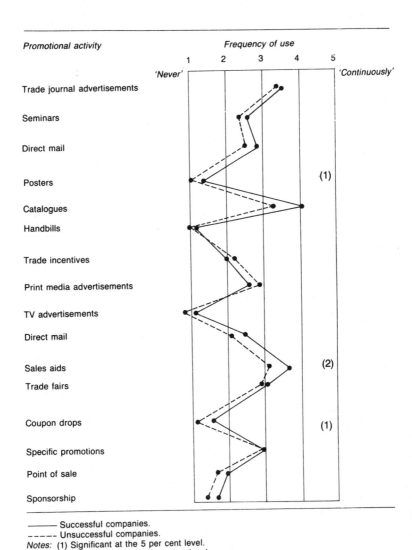

Figure 6.12 Promotional Activity in Successful and Less Successful
Companies

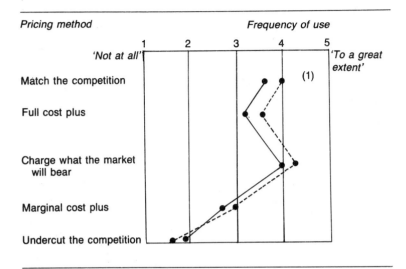

Pricing method   Frequency of use

——— Successful companies.
– – – – Unsuccessful companies.
Note: (1) Significant at the 5 per cent level.

Figure 6.13 Pricing in Successful and Less Successful Companies

Reprise

Of the various tactical factors investigated, the more successful companies were more actively involved in market research and information gathering, market segmentation and promotion. The above-average performers carried out more in-house market research and employed more external agencies for specific studies. They conducted more customer surveys and field experiments than the below-average performers. The successful companies collated more types of internal information; they monitored stock levels, operational problems and the contribution of each product to overall sales volume to a far greater extent than the less successful companies. While there is little conclusive evidence to support the contention that successful companies segment their markets more than the less successful companies, as is shown by Figure 6.11, successful companies were more active in most methods of segmentation than less successful ones.

Finally, while both above- and below-average performers claimed to engage in promotional activity, the former used sponsorship, catalogues, coupon drops, point-of-sale material, posters and sales aids to a far greater degree than the latter.

On a number of marketing tactics, very little difference between the two groups of companies was detected. In some instances — distribution, for example — the precise nature of a company's operations seems to be imposed by the structure of the market.

6.5 Conclusion

The findings described in this chapter highlight those areas where there are differences in the policies and practices between above- and below-average companies. Specifically, differences relate to the *structure* of the companies, the *strategies*, and to the *tasks*, employed to pursue the strategies.

At the structural level, however, the existence of particular departments or Board titles is as much related to size as any other factor. In other words, it is impossible to look at obvious indicators of commitment to marketing. It is therefore necessary to look at more subtle factors, like the extent to which marketing personnel communicate with top-level decision makers, or the extent to which there is a clear and defined *responsibility* for marketing.

At the *strategic* level, the studies identified a few factors that seem to distinguish between above- and below-average companies: a long-term approach, specific strategic objectives, linking strategic plans closely with changes in markets, and a continuous commitment to new product development are all activities apparent in *more* successful companies rather than *less* successful ones.

At the *tactical* level, market research, market segmentation, and certain promotional techniques are more common in successful companies.

Overall, it is possible to say that relatively few of the factors studied actually accounted for differences in performance. However, the fact that these tightly-controlled studies failed to find more factors which distinguish the successful from the less successful is, in itself, very important. Both studies covered a wide range of issues, from the McKinsey '7-S' framework and the simultaneous loose—tight structures of Peters and Waterman

(1982) to the managerial style reported as being important by Saunders and Wong (1985). It seems, therefore, that our findings lend force to early criticisms of studies purporting to identify correlates of success in high-performance companies. As the data show, the firms in our sample — which are all successful given that they survived the recession of the early 1980s — tend to be similar in terms of their policies and practices. That this is so is hardly surprising: books like *In Search of Excellence* and *A Passion for Excellence* are successful *because* managers are anxious to adopt those procedures and practices recommended as giving rise to improved competitive performance. Indeed, we would predict that, if our findings are disseminated widely, the few factors that distinguish successful companies from less successful ones will cease to do so in a few years because more companies will have picked them up and adopted them too.

When a given factor is universally applied, its use as a discriminator is at an end. Clearly, discriminators are much more subtle than earlier commentators would have us believe. Perhaps Ames (1970) was closest to the truth when he drew attention to the difference between the *substance* and the *trappings* of marketing. Certainly, our findings lend support to the old adage, 'it's not what you do, it's the way that you do it'.

Appendix

Those *figures* based on t-tests are:
6.3, 6.4, 6.5, 6.7, 6.8, 6.9, 6.10, 6.12, 6.13.

Those *figures* based on chi-square tests are:
6.1, 6.6, 6.11.

Those *tables* based on chi-square tests are:
6.3, 6.4, 6.6, 6.7, 6.8, 6.14, 6.15

Table 6.13 is based on the Mann–Whitney U test.

References

Alexander, M. (1985) 'Creative marketing and innovative consumer product decision — some case studies' *Design Studies*, vol. 6, no. 1, January.

Ames, B.C. (1970) 'Trappings versus substance in industrial marketing', *Harvard Business Review*, vol. 48, July/August.

Ansoff, I. (1968) *Corporate Strategy*, Penguin Books.

Bruce, M. (1985) 'The design process and the "crisis" in the UK information technology industry', *Design Studies*, vol. 6, no. 1.

Challis, H. (1983) 'Teaming up with design', *Engineer's Digest*, vol. 44, no. 11.

Doyle, P., Saunders, J. and Wong, V. (1985) *A Comparative Investigation of Japanese Marketing Strategies in the British Market*, Report to ESRC.

Hayes, R. and Abernathy, W. (1980) 'Managing our way to economic decline', *Harvard Business Review*, July/August.

Hooley, G. and Lynch, J. (1985) 'Marketing lessons from UK's high-flying companies', *Journal of Marketing Management*, vol. 1, no. 1, Summer.

King, S. (1985) 'Has marketing failed or was it never really tried?', *Journal of Marketing Management*, vol. 1, no. 2, Summer.

Peters, T.J. and Waterman, R.W. (1982) *In Search of Excellence*, Harper & Row.

Piercy, N. (1985) 'The role and function of the chief marketing executive and the marketing department — a study of medium-sized companies in the UK', *Journal of Marketing Management*, vol. 1, no. 3, Spring.

Porter, M.E. (1980) *Competitive Strategy: Techniques for Analysing Industries as Competitors*, The Free Press.

Rothwell, R. *et al*. (1974) 'Project SAPPHO updated — Project SAPPHO Phase II', *Research Policy*, 3.

Saunders, J. and Wong, V. (1985) 'In search of excellence in the UK', *Journal of Marketing Management*, vol. 1, no. 2, Winter.

Walsh, V. and Roy, R. (1983) *Plastics Products: Good Design, Innovation and Business Success*, The Open University, Design Innovation Group DIG-01, August.

Webster, F.E. (1981) 'Top managements concerns about marketing: issues for the 1980s', *Journal of Marketing*, vol. 45, Summer, pp. 9–16.

7

The Search for Quality

In light of the findings of the research reported in the previous chapter it will be helpful here to review the themes and issues addressed in this book prior to drawing conclusions and offering recommendations in the final chapter. In essence, the studies reported in Chapter 6 were a direct response to a series of basic assumptions and propositions which may be summarised as follows:

1. There has been a continuing and significant decline in the UK's international competitiveness which has accelerated markedly over the past 25 years. The decline is apparent in both the penetration of the UK home market by imports and in our rapidly dwindling share of international trade – particularly in manufactured goods, in which Britain used to dominate.

2. It is the declared objective of all political parties to improve the standard of living of the British population. Irrespective of their political philosophy for achieving this, it is essential that UK Limited improve its competitiveness and international trading performance in order to generate the wealth to pay for this improved standard of living.

3. To be able to improve competitiveness, one must first identify and diagnose those factors which underlie our declining performance as the basis for developing policies, strategies and plans to reverse the trend.

4. Preliminary analysis reveals that our declining competitiveness is attributable to a multiplicity of factors which may be conveniently classified into four groups:

   - Environmental/technological   • Strategic
   - Attitudinal/structural   • Managerial

161

5. Analysis of these factors has led to a number of highly
    publicised statements of 'critical success factors' and 'corre-
    lates of success' in books such as *In Search of Excellence, The
    Winning Streak* and *A Passion for Excellence*.
6. However, many commentators have criticised these
    analyses, and their proposals for improved performance,
    on the grounds that they were methodologically flawed
    in a variety of ways. They are usually cross-sectional and
    examine 'success' at a point in time when they should be
    longitudinal, monitoring performance over a period of
    years — for example, several of Peters and Waterman's
    'excellent firms' were in distinct difficulty only a year or
    two after they had been held up as exemplars for all to
    emulate. A second major flaw in the methodology was that
    by concentrating analysis upon currently successful firms
    the researchers overlooked the fact that many of the
    policies and practices advocated as critical success factors
    were also present in less successful and unsuccessful firms,
    indicating that a more sophisticated explanation was
    required than, say, the presence of a strategic planning
    function or a marketing department.

In the light of these propositions, the structure of the book was
designed to establish:

- factual evidence of the decline in UK competitiveness, in
  terms of both export sales and import penetration *(Chapter 1)*;
- a review of the reasons why specialisation and exchange lead
  to increased productivity and a higher standard of living,
  or satisfaction, for all those involved *(Chapter 2)*;
- an evaluation of the popular view that change is revolutionary — epitomised by reference to 'accelerating change',
  'turbulence', the 'knowledge-based society', etc. — when
  a longer perspective clearly indicates that change is evolutionary and that valuable lessons can be learned by
  reviewing past experience *(Chapter 3)*;
- a comprehensive and critical evaluation of current views and
  ideas on the sources and nature of competitive advantage
  and success — this confirmed that current prescriptions for
  success are based on partial data (that is, they have failed
  to establish that the success factors are absent in less success-

ful or unsuccessful companies) — and propose courses of action which are difficult to operationalise *(Chapter 4)*;
- a report of research which would address the methodological weaknesses of earlier studies based upon a simple but robust model of the sources of competitiveness, derived from the literature review *(Chapter 5)*;
- a description of the findings of the research — this revealed that many critical success factors are present in less successful companies, so that it is the quality of execution which differentiates between different levels of performance *(Chapter 6)*.

The question is, therefore, 'What defines and determines quality and how do we set about achieving it?' In this chapter we will seek to answer the first part of the question, leaving the second part to be answered in the final chapter.

7.1 Knowledge and Understanding

While knowledge can be communicated relatively easily, understanding is more difficult to achieve. If it were not so then all one need do to succeed would be to read and memorise the definitive book on military strategy to become a general, on chess to become a chessmaster, on painting to become a famous artist, and so on. So it is with management books — one can observe successful companies and describe what they do and how their managers behave but one cannot 'make' successful managers merely by communicating knowledge as to what successful managers do. Because 'wisdom can't be told' the Harvard Business School exposes its MBA students to over 1,000 case studies of real-world business situations in just the same way that teaching hospitals require interns to accompany skilled practitioners so that their knowledge of the symptoms of illness and its cure can be refined into an understanding which is essential to effective practice. Of course, variations in innate ability will still remain, but without understanding, improvement is unlikely.

In order to understand why current competitive conditions appear to call for new managerial approaches, it is important first to know what factors have led to this current situation. Basically, competition is all about the interaction of supply and demand in the market-place. But, while economists have developed sophisticated abstract models of this interaction, these fail to capture the richness and dynamism of the real world, in which individuals and firms decline to behave in the limited and stable manner predicted by the theory. As a result, practitioners frequently dismiss theory as a source of understanding and behave as if each situation is wholly unique, so that knowledge of previous occurrences and outcomes can shed little or no light on the problems which face them. To do so is to ignore the fact that while problems may vary in the particular, there are a number of basic underlying relationships which, if understood, provide a framework for diagnosis of the specific problem. As we saw in Chapter 3 (pp. 33–38), there is a spectrum of competitive states ranging from pure competition to monopoly, each of which is defined by the prevailing relationship between demand and supply. If, therefore, we are to understand competition, it would seem reasonable to claim that one must first understand the fundamental nature of these underlying forces.

7.2 Demand

In the absence of demand, an output or supply has no value. It would seem reasonable, therefore, to claim that the existence of demand predisposes entrepreneurs to combine factors of production in order to create specific supplies, such that demand is the motivating and driving force which dictates what shall be supplied, when, and in what quantities. If this is so, then an understanding of competition clearly must begin with an understanding of what creates demand.

Fundamentally, demand is derived from human needs, although purists would probably wish to draw a distinction between 'physiological needs' essential for survival and 'wants' which reflect individual preferences for satisfying these needs as modified by economic, sociological and psychological factors. It was to reflect the mediating influence of other factors that Abraham Maslow (1943) developed his concept of the *need hierarchy* in 1943. This is a simple and robust model which has stood the test of time, and it provides a sound basis for understanding what motivates consumers to 'demand' particular goods and services. Maslow's model recognises five stages which, in ascending order of importance, may be defined as follows:

1. *Physiological:* the fundamentals of survival, including hunger and thirst.
2. *Safety:* concern over physical survival and safety which might be overcome in satisfying physiological needs.
3. *Belongingness and love:* the need to be accepted by one's immediate family and to be important to them.
4. *Esteem and status:* the need to achieve a 'high standing', relative to others outside the immediate family; the desire for mastery, reputation and prestige.
5. *Self-actualisation:* desire to know, understand, systematise and construct a system of values.

Symbolically the hierarchy is usually depicted as a pyramid as in Figure 7.1.

In essence, then, Maslow is proposing three levels of need: (i) survival, (ii) human interaction and involvement and (iii) competency and self-esteem, with higher-order motives usually lying

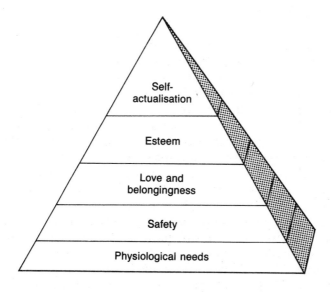

Figure 7.1 Maslow's Hierarchy of Needs

dormant until the lower levels are satisfied. There are, of course, exceptions to this generalisation and ample evidence that individuals at the highest level can sublimate lower-order motives, for example Gandhi and hunger strikers. That said, the model does reflect that throughout history mankind has aspired to higher levels of satisfaction than those in the temporal, physical and material domains. To a significant degree their success in doing so has been constrained by their productivity or ability to create 'supply' which, in turn, has depended upon organisational and technological development.

7.3   Socio-economic Evolution

To a large extent, the ability of individuals to progress to the pinnacle of their personal need hierarchy is conditioned by social and economic factors — social in terms of the way in which people organise their collective activity, and economic in terms of the success which they achieve in addressing the central economic problem of maximising satisfaction through the utilisation of scarce resources. A synoptic and eclectic review of economic history may help to establish the proposition that while some individuals have always been able to achieve the higher levels of the need hierarchy, it is only in recent times that a significant proportion of the total population has been able to aspire to the top two levels.

While physiological needs are intensely personal, groups are virtually an essential prerequisite for the achievement of safety and love needs. Once groups are established, it becomes clear that collective action and social organisation will lead to increased productivity and welfare: first, through task specialisation; and second, through the division of labour. The first is admirably exemplified by the medieval craft gilds and the second by Adam Smith's classic example of the pin-making industry.

Smith noted that where men were engaged in all processes involved in the manufacture of pins, their average output was 20 pins per day; when the manufacture of pins was broken down into separate processes output for the group rose to 4,000 pins per man per day. Two points are of particular significance in this step forward. First, organisation, or 'management', is required to bring together the men, provide a place of work and supply raw materials. Second, the enormous increase in output reduces the price of the commodity, necessitates the development of channels of distribution to make the article available to those with a demand for it, and leads to a significant increase in consumer welfare.

However, the real potential of task specialisation and the division of labour can only be realised when harnessed to techno-logical innovation – of the kind initiated by the scientific break-throughs of the Renaissance, the Age of Enlightenment and the Industrial Revolution – and transferred into commercial products by the craftsmen and artisans of the period. In turn, new materials, methods and machines greatly increase the scope for further discovery and so lend further impetus to the accelerating rate of change with which we are now so familiar. But, while the spirit of inquiry may have lent force to the enormous rate of economic development experienced in the past 200 years, there can be no doubt that the real catalyst was the existence of market opportunities, for it is these which transform speculative inventions into profitable innovations.

Consequently, market opportunities reflected both the growth of population, which was, itself, a consequence of improved standards of living resulting in greater productivity, and the aspirations of individuals to move up their own personal need hierarchies. But, what happens if, for whatever reason, supply exceeds demand? Until comparatively recently, such a question would have been viewed as hypothetical and probably absurd. Yet much of our recent economic (and managerial) history has been dominated by this issue, as the perception of a levelling-off of demand (growth) has led to increased competition and the turbulent economic conditions which have prompted managerial concern for more effective competitive strategies. However, this is not a new phenomenon. This possibility was experienced, at a national level, by a number of countries towards the end of the last century, and it is epitomised by Robert Reich's (1984) analysis and description of what he calls 'the era of management' as a response to a problem which has been characterised as 'overproduction'.

The explosion in productive capacity that marked the first decades of America's industrialisation soon outpassed the nation's ability to distribute, market, and consume all the new output. Firms had energetically built up capacity, despite the fact that their rivals were doing the same. As supply burgeoned, producers anxious to sell enough to recover the cost of their new factories turned to cut-throat competition. Prices declined. The wholesale price index, which had stood at 193 in 1864, had dropped to 82 by 1890. A major depression jolted the economy in 1893, impoverishing entire agricultural areas, closing thousands of banks, and throwing more than one-fourth of the unskilled urban labour force out of jobs. [Shades of the 1970s!]

The immediate reaction in the USA was to follow the German example and form cartels. But, lacking the existence of a large public bureaucracy which was able to exercise control over cartels (as in Germany), Americans viewed cartelisation as illegitimate and passed the Sherman Anti-trust legislation which prohibited them. Mergers and acquisitions followed (shades of the 1980s) and, where they led to economies of scale — such as in US Steel, General Electric and Standard Oil — they resulted in survival and then success.

However, the emergence of the mega-corporation exaggerated a problem which had already begun to be felt in the earliest stages of industrialisation — the management of people. It was this which resulted in the twentieth century becoming the era of management (Reich 1984).

Management emerged around 1920 as a philosophy, a science, and a pervasive metaphor which would dominate the way Americans viewed themselves and their institutions for the next fifty years.

Management was America's own creation. No other industrialised nation so fully embraced it or experienced its spectacular capacity to generate new wealth.

The paradigm of management served to dominate its time. Many of the problems that emerged in America before World War I — within its factories, among its enterprises, and in society at large — had been rooted, in bottlenecks, inefficiencies, poor coordination and inadequate controls. The managerial ideas and institutions that arose after the war solved many of these problems. They bore for America the fruits of high-volume, standardised production. The managed organisation replicated itself across the country — in businesses, government agencies, and labour unions — promising stability, order, and prosperity. For fifty years it faithfully delivered.

Reich's review of the era of management deserves careful consideration, particularly in terms of the three cardinal principles of scientific management – specialisation through simplification, predetermined rules and the detailed monitoring of performance. Task specialisation has already been referred to, but its full potential was only realised with the birth of a new race of time-and-motion specialists. But once the job had been broken down in the minutest detail, few (if any) workers had much conception of how their own contribution meshed with that of adjacent tasks, let alone the overall operation. To ensure the necessary coordination, explicit rules and close supervision through a managerial hierarchy became essential. To ensure it was being exercised both efficiently and effectively, management information was a necessity.

7.4 Managerial Orientation

While Reich's concern is largely with the nature of the managerial task and its execution, our concern lies more with the underlying motivation or orientation of management. While facing the risk of gross over-simplification it would seem that one can distinguish three or possibly four basic managerial orientations which have dominated the organisation of production and distribution.

The first and least apparent approach to management may be labelled *Collection*, which is typical of the traditional nomadic societies who eke out a survival existence. The limitations on such societies are painfully obvious to us all in the famines which have blighted Africa in recent years. To improve welfare and exercise a degree of control over the environment one needs a more sophisticated approach, and this may be characterised as a *Production* orientation which, as we have seen, is made possible by task specialisation, the division of labour and industrialisation. Its zenith is represented by Taylor's scientific management and it is clearly the most appropriate response when demand exceeds supply. Under such conditions the nature of demand tends to be fairly self-evident, and the ultimate objective of maximising satisfaction is best realised by producing the 'mostest for the leastest'. But consider again what happens if the capacity to produce exceeds the ability to consume?

As we have seen, such conditions developed in the USA (and elsewhere) towards the end of the last century and led to recession. They also occurred in the 1920s and again in the 1970s. The immediate response to the recession of the 1890s was a reorganisation of production which both reduced direct competition of the kind which economists misguidedly term 'perfect' and enhanced the efficiency of those who survived the shake out. In the 1920s (and the 1970s) similar responses are apparent, as is the emergence of a switch in emphasis from a production to a sales orientation. Under a sales orientation, the producer is still concerned to sell what he can make, but under the pressures of competition he realises he must take an active rather than a passive interest in his potential customer and so invests considerable effort in seeking to ensure his patronage. It is this pressure to encourage us to consume more which has attracted such adverse criticism of high-pressure selling and 'the age of high mass consumption'.

Selling has been, and always will be, an essential management function. It is not a sound basis for orientating a business in the long run because its essence is to *push* products at customers, when the preferred status is to have customers *pull* products through channels of production and distribution. It was recognition of this which led to the emergence of the marketing concept and its attendant marketing orientation. Of course, marketing is not new – every successful entrepreneur since time immemorial has been good at marketing, even if he didn't know of its existence. The problem is that with increasing competition and stagnating demand success does not come so easily. Products are infinitely more complex, consumers are better educated and informed, and the production and consumption functions in society have become separated by elaborate channels of distribution. Clearly, to succeed nowadays, producers need to re-establish contact with their markets and take the trouble to find out what consumers really want – an orientation to the market rather than a preoccupation with the factory.

7.5 Coalescing Trends

While it is potentially misleading to represent managerial orientations as a hierarchy like Maslow's, we have suggested elsewhere (Baker 1987 – on which this section draws heavily) that currently we can discern a number of coalescing trends which can be represented symbolically, as in Figure 7.2. Similarly, it will be useful to represent, in a similar fashion, the stages of economic and technological evolution touched on earlier. In the case of the stages of economic growth, we already possess Rostow's well-known model reproduced in Figure 7.3, while the organisational/technological stages of development might appear as in Figure 7.4.

If these models are combined, as in Figure 7.5, we can see that the age of high mass-consumption, made possible by high technology, stimulated by selling and epitomised by esteem (*keeping up with the Jones'*) have all come together in the post World War II era. Maslow tells us that the stage beyond esteem is self-actualisation, and as consumers become more individualistic we shall need a marketing orientation in order to define clearly and satisfy their particular needs. But what about the 'stages of economic growth'? − *beyond high mass consumption*, like *post-industrial society*, is not a particularly helpful descriptor. Rostow himself recognised this and in a revision of his model, the apex (formerly *beyond high mass-consumption*) was re-labelled *the search for quality* (Figure 7.6) − the theme of this chapter.

But we still have one space unfilled. What comes after *high technology*? In fact, it is not so much what comes after high technology, for all the indications are that it will continue to evolve. As Alvin Toffler (1971) has pointed out, it is the progress of high technology which has brought us to the point where self-actualisation, customisation and quality are all within our grasp.

> Take 'mass production'. Nothing was more characteristic of the industrial era. Yet we're already moving from a mass-production, mass-consumption economy to what I've called a 'de-massified' economy.
> In traditional mass manufacturing, factories pour out a stream of identical objects, by the million. In the Third Wave sector, mass production is replaced by its opposite: de-massified production − short runs, even customized, one-by-one production, based on computers and numerical controls. Even where we turn out millions of identical components, they are frequently configured into more and more customized end products.
> The significance of this can't be overestimated. It's not simply that producers are now more varied. The processes of production are themselves transformed. The smoke-stack − that symbol of the industrial assembly-line society − is becoming a relic.

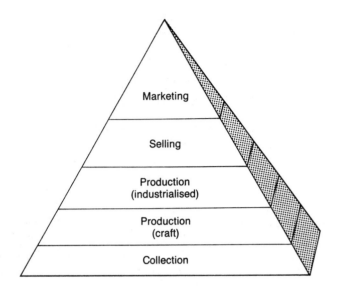

Figure 7.2 Managerial Orientations

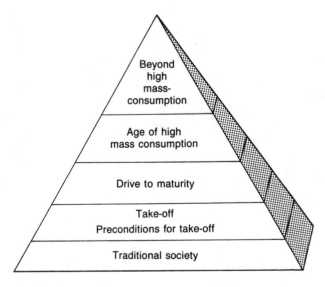

Figure 7.3 Rostow's Stages of Economic Growth

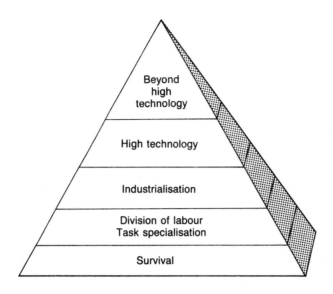

Figure 7.4 Organisational/technological Stages of Development

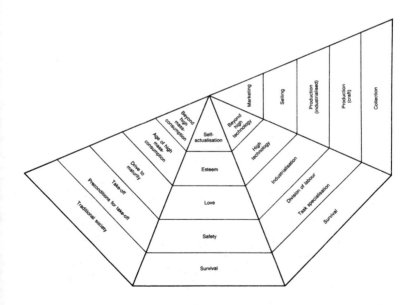

Figure 7.5 Coalescing Trends: I

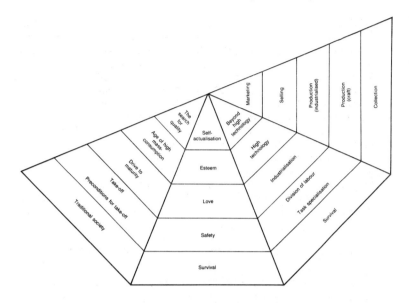

Figure 7.6 Coalescing Trends: II

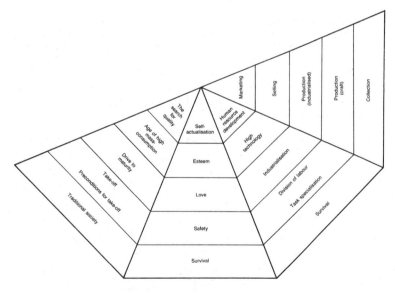

Figure 7.7 Coalescing Trends: III

We still think of ourselves as a mass production society, yet in the advanced sectors of the economy, mass production is already an outmoded technique. And the idea that we can keep our old mass manufacturing industries competitive indefinitely is based on ignorance of what is actually happening on the factory floor.

The new techniques make diversity as cheap as uniformity. In fact, in many industries, it's customize or die. This is exactly the opposite of what was required in the Second Wave economy.

In fact, it is almost a dialectical return to pre-industrial, one-of-a-kind production, but now on a high technology basis.

And exactly the same trends are visible in the distribution system, too, where we see more and more market segmentation, direct mail targeting, speciality stores, and even individualized delivery systems based on home computers and teleshopping. People are increasingly diverse and, as a result, the mass market is breaking into small, continually changing sectors.

The real challenge is whether we will be able to respond to the opportunity which burgeoning technology offers to us. This is the question addressed by Reich in *The Next American Frontier*, in which he proposes that the next step in our socio-economic and political evolution has to be 'the era of human capital'.

As citizens we must transcend the old categories of civil culture and business culture and recognise the relationship between the nation's social and economic development. Americans concerned with social justice must become familiar with the subtleties of American business and recognise the importance of profit seeking and investment in economic growth. American businessmen must accept that claims for participation and fairness are not obstacles to their mission, but ultimately its very substance. [For 'American' read 'world'.]

If we are to break through the constraints which appear to inhibit our progress, we must seek quality not quantity as our aspiration. In pursuit of quality, we must recognise that it is the needs of the individual which are paramount. But, to deliver the quality and variety called for and expected by today's discerning and affluent customers, 'human capital' must be seen as the source of competitive advantage. Accordingly, we may complete the model by adding to it *human resource development* (see Figure 7.7). In turn, human resource development is very much a question of corporate culture and it is to this issue that we turn in the final chapter.

References

Baker, M.J. (1987) (ed.) *The Marketing Book*, Heinemann.
Maslow, A. (1943) 'A theory of human motivation', *Psychological Review*, vol. 50.
Reich, R. (1984) *The Next American Frontier*, Penguin Books.
Rostow, W.N. (1962) *The Stages of Economic Growth*, Cambridge University Press.
Toffler, Alvin (1971) *Future Shock*, Bodley Head.

8

Developing a Competitive Culture

8.1 Declining Competitiveness

The focus of this book has been upon UK firms, UK experiences and ultimately the health of the UK economy, but one must be careful not to assume that we are alone in the problems which we face. In 1984 Harvard Business School Professor Bruce Scott pointed out that the US economy faced similar problems of declining competitiveness. In 1950 the USA accounted for 6 per cent of the world's population, 40 per cent of its GNP and 20 per cent of world trade. Thirty years later, in 1979, the statistics were 5 per cent of world population, 21.5 per cent of GNP and 11 per cent of its trade. Scott observed: 'Since the mid-1960s, the profitability of US companies has declined and for the last decade the return on manufacturing assets has hardly been above that of corporate bonds. Loss of market share and profitability over a sustained period signal an unmistakable decline in competitiveness'. In the 4 years since Scott identified the decline in US competitiveness, its international trade balance has worsened and was a major issue in the 1988 presidential election campaigns. What, then, was Scott's diagnosis and prognosis, and to what extent, if any, have his prescriptions for change been followed?

Then, as now, many mainstream economists, including those advising the President, considered that the decline in the US share of GNP and exports was only to be expected, given the abnormal economic conditions which prevailed after World War II. In the view of these economists, one must examine the composition of trade to determine whether this reflects the theory of comparative advantage which would require the USA to increase exports of high-technology products, resource intensive products other than fuels, and foreign investment while accepting imports of less sophisticated products with a high raw material and labour content, like textiles. This, in fact, was the case and led analysts to argue that it was an overvalued dollar which was responsible for the negative trade balance. However, as Scott pointed out, this was only a partial explanation because the symptoms of declining competitiveness were apparent between 1973 and 1979 when the dollar floated down and was considered undervalued. In Scott's view (and that of many other current observers) the problem is much more serious and arises from an inability to cut social spending. This had risen due to cuts in defence spending under the Democrats, in line with increased spending on defence introduced in 1978 which was not funded through increased taxation.

A second school of thought attributed declining competitiveness to industrial mismanagement, maintaining that, 'many leading corporations have become complacent, have paid inadequate attention to product quality and to product and process innovation, have over-emphasised short-term earnings, and have produced a new school of management aptly labelled "paper entrepreneurship" ' (Scott, *op.cit*). While systematic evidence of these charges is hard to marshal, they comprise the starting point for many of the studies of competitiveness with a corporate or microeconomic perspective, including those reviewed in Chapter 4.

Yet another school of thought, possibly influenced by the role of MITI (Ministry of International Trade and Industry) in Japan's economic revival, attributes falling competitiveness to the absence of an explicit industrial policy designed to ease the problems of declining industries while offering greater assistance to the new high-technology industries. Scott pointed out that 'many industrial policy proponents ignore the fact that our [US] government has no mechanism to formulate an explicit industrial policy and no clearly accepted role other than that of referee of marketplace competition'. Nonetheless, this school of thought finds most favour with Scott who argues that it offers hope for improvement, but only if any new economic strategy is firmly founded upon a true understanding of the nature of international competition. In Scott's view, this indicates that it is to the Far

East that the USA must look, not to its traditional European rivals, for their performance — even when based upon an articulated industrial policy — has not improved when compared with that of the USA.

Scott believes that: 'The malaise of North Atlantic industrial companies has four main causes: a less favourable world economic environment, new competition, the targeting policies of some governments, and the general anti-industrial bias of our present economic strategy'. Specifically, these four facts may be summarised as:

1. A *less favourable economic climate* due to lower growth, successive oil price shocks and the monetary squeeze from October 1979 to August 1982.
2. *New competition* arising from declining trade barriers, shrinking transport costs and improvements in communications which have facilitated global competition and worldwide product sourcing.
3. *Industrial targeting* whereby governments and industry collaborate to identify and promote key industries and technologies providing a competitive edge over those which do not — for example, Japan, France and several NICs (Newly Industrialising Countries) versus the USA and the UK, where the 'invisible hand' of market forces prevails. That said, Scott believes that it is not targeting which makes the difference, but rather its incorporation into an aggressive overall strategy.
4. The *anti-industrial ethos* is not defined explicitly but may be inferred as consisting of an anti-business bias focused on issues of environmentalism, consumerism, social responsibility and the like, coupled with a failure to recognise that consumer welfare benefits must be paid for from added value somewhere in the economy.

At the national level, however, Scott's analysis reveals a situation very similar to that documented by Rothwell and his colleagues for the UK — namely, a loss of market share in world markets for high-technology products in which, the theory of comparative advantage argues, it should be improving its position. In fact, as of the early 1980s, only Japan appears to have increased its share of high technology markets while withdrawing from low technology markets — an achievement which 'High-level Japanese officials . . . explain as the result of their rejection of the static theory of comparative advantage . . . . In its place . . . they have developed a notion of dynamic comparative advantage' (Scott, *op. cit.*).

The concept of dynamic comparative advantage, as perceived by Scott, rejects the assumption central to economic theory of diminishing marginal returns (increased costs) with continuing rises in output. 'While the proposition holds in the short run, abundant evidence indicates that in the long run costs decline indefinitely in real terms, partly from increasing returns to scale and partly because users learn to be more efficient'. This phenomenon of the experience curve applied particularly in high technology industries and is well known to and accepted by managers. But in Scott's view its existence is regarded as anecdotal by economists and has not made its way into economic theory with the result that economists still promote a concept of comparative advantage which encourages massive import penetration and widespread unemployment.

By contrast, the Japanese rejected the superficial implications of a static theory of comparative advantage, which would have directed them towards labour-intensive industries, and chose instead to concentrate upon industries 'in which technical change and rising productivity could yield declining unit costs'.

In essence, the static theory of comparative advantage represents a short-term tactical response, whereas the dynamic theory requires one to look ahead and identify tomorrow's winners (growth industries) rather than concentrate upon today's cash cows. Once the future opportunities for growth have been identified, the firm (or nation) can begin to acquire the resources and skills necessary to succeed in that market. Whether or not it has a natural comparative advantage is of secondary importance as, in the absence of active competition, the initial costs of entry, together with the acquisition of experience, will be much less costly than will be the case when the advantages of entry are obvious to all.

At the national level (the focus of Scott's paper), the question is whether countries can depend upon the 'invisible hand' to remove the veil which clouds the vision of individual investors, firms or industries, or whether purposive action, in the form of a government–business dialogue and an industrial policy, is required. Japan's success suggests it is the latter, but simultaneously raises the questions of unity of purpose and continuity. In the UK, adversarial politics dependent upon polarised policies have resulted in a stop–go approach to the management of the economy which has acted as a strong deterrent to the long-term 'visionary' attitude which underpinned our original commercial success as a trading nation and appears to be vital to the acquisition of 'experience' and the benefits which flow from it.

During the past decade, consistent industrial policy, together with increasing competitive pressure from both industrialised and less-developed countries, has encouraged a return to the entrepreneurial approach of the nineteenth-century pioneers. Thus, it becomes clear that attitudinal factors embraced in concepts like 'business confidence' and 'corporate culture' will have an important role to play in determining both the process of strategy formulation and the quality of implementation.

8.2 Competitiveness and Performance Improvement

Faced with declining competitiveness of the kind chronicled in earlier chapters, it is clear that managers in advanced, Western industrialised countries must achieve a significant improvement in performance if they are to survive the 'new competition', particularly from Japan and the Far East. In very simple terms, performance may be regarded as the outcome of the interaction between knowledge and skills (discussed in Chapter 7) as mediated by attitudes, i.e.

$$P = f(K, S, A)$$

where P = Performance
 f = a function of
 K = Knowledge
 S = Skills
 A = Attitudes

We speak of knowledge, skills and attitudes (KSA) in that order because it reflects the fact of normal human development. Society perceives education as the most cost-effective means of transferring knowledge, which is the distillation of past experience, from one generation to the next. In order to put knowledge into practice we are trained to acquire skills of implementation, and our perception of the preferred or 'best' method will depend very much upon the value systems of the society in which the knowledge and skills are acquired. It is this latter which leads to the formation of attitudes which may be defined as 'a predisposition to act' — that is, faced with a problem, attitudes will influence both our perception of the problem and the preferred courses of action. However, it is this sequence which also leads to the phenomenon which we term 'resistance to change', since, once we have acquired knowledge and skills, proposals for change require that we modify or even discard the very knowledge and skills which we have worked so hard to acquire. Small wonder that the prevailing attitude is one of resistance to actions which would diminish our 'human capital'.

If, therefore, we want to improve performance, perhaps we need to restate our simple model as:

$$PI = f[A\ (K,\ S)]$$

In other words, Performance Improvement (*PI*) will only come about if we can first accomplish an attitudinal change which will encourage individuals, and particularly managers, to review and reassess their current stock of knowledge and skills. In turn, the first step towards attitude modification must be awareness of the existence of a problem which, in the present context, has been defined and described in terms of diminishing international competitiveness. In the case of senior managers in industry, the problems which they face are typically those which:

- are less structured and more ill-defined;
- are more complex and contain many variables;
- involve greater uncertainty;
- demand more judgement; and
- have higher consequences.

As we have seen, in recent years these characteristics have become exaggerated due to the combined effects of increased international competition stimulated by accelerating technological change. And, while we have argued that these changes and the accompanying turbulence are no different in *kind* from previous organisational and technological 'revolutions', there can be no doubt that the *degree* or *intensity* of change called for in the past 20 years has been more acute than in the past. As a consequence, the environment faced by managers is significantly different from that which prevailed in the immediate postwar period when most of the CEOs of major corporations were acquiring their managerial knowledge and skills. Clearly, it is the attitudes of these CEOs which will largely determine the thrust and direction of their organisations now, so that the first step to improving performance and competitiveness must be to ask what is their perception of the environment and the issues which they face?

In the early 1980s a survey of top European CEOs identified eight factors which characterise the environment facing management, namely:

  (i) a demand for quality and advice;
 (ii) a move towards a service culture;
(iii) an emphasis upon the specialist;
 (iv) shortening strategic time horizons;
  (v) scenario planning replacing forecasting;
 (vi) a reduction in head-office functions;
(vii) a wider international outlook;
(viii) tighter legislation.

The first three trends were discussed at some length in the preceding chapter, *The Search for Quality*. Shortening strategic time horizons are, of course, a direct consequence of accelerating technological change and improved communication such that it is now estimated that any new technology will be fully known around the world within eighteen months of its first appearance. Given such rapid change, conventional forecasting — using extrapolation of past trends — is of little value in predicting the future, and more broadly-based scenarios become necessary to help chart future direction.

The reduction in head-office functions is a trend which began to develop in the early 1980s when CEOs came to realise that one of the causes which had led to a poor response to the recession and acute competition of the late 1970s was that by devolving responsibility for key functions to staff officers they had lost contact with the market-place and so were ill-placed to take early remedial action. As a consequence of this recognition, there has been a marked reduction in the size and number of formal strategic planning and marketing departments. Operational responsibility for these functions is now embedded in the operating divisions while strategic responsibility has been re-assumed by CEOs, aided by small advisory staffs.

A wider international outlook is a natural and necessary reaction to the realities of competition. Finally, tighter legislation is a direct response both to consumer sovereignty and its demand for quality and value for money and to the pressures of international competition and the emergence of economic groupings like the EEC.

One company's response to these changes is encapsulated in Philip's 'World Vision', stated as the basis for a reformulation of their corporate strategy. The key factors identified by Philip may be summarised as:

1. The world is diminishing in size.
2. Turbulence is shaking-up and shaking-out the old order.
3. Technology and change are pushing the organisation to its limits and beyond.
4. The scale of technological development is beyond the resources of all but the very largest organisation.
5. Distribution has come to dominate manufacturing.
6. Customers are becoming even more demanding.
7. Politics is exerting more influence on trade, production, employment and finance.

These, and other similar analyses, point unequivocally to the fact that we are moving to a post-industrial 'Information Era' which exhibits the following shifts:

From	To
Standardisation	→ Customisation
Centralisation	→ Decentralisation
Dependence	→ Selp-help
Transportation	→ Communication
Autocracy	→ Participation
Hierarchy	→ Network
Information Scarcity	→ Information overload

Given these trends what must the organisation do if it is not only to survive but also to prosper?

8.3 The Quest for Success

Perhaps the first thing the organisation must recognise is that
while it is confronted by a rapidly-changing environment, the real
determinant of its success is how it performs within the industry
markets in which it is a player. This is so because the external
environment is common to all of the competitors within a given
industry and so offers the same threats and opportunities to them
all. Of course, this is not to say that all members of an industry
will be equally good at reading the signals from the external
environment with the obvious corollary that those who are better
at environmental analysis will enjoy a competitive edge over their
rivals. But, as Michael Porter (1980) has demonstrated so convincingly, it is the 'jockeying for position' within an industry
which is the real determinant of success. (In the long run, of
course, it is hoped that one could switch capital from mature and
declining industries with low returns into new, growth industries
with higher returns. In the short to medium term, however, one
must make the best of the situation one is in which will also determine the value of the capital and assets to be transferred into
newer, more promising areas).

In an article which anticipated the publication of his book,
Porter (1979) proposed a simple model of the forces governing
competition within an industry, which is reproduced as Figure
8.1.

Leaving aside the external forces which impact upon all
members of the industry, Porter distinguishes eight factors which
influence the intensity of rivalry between competitors within an
industry, namely:

1. Numerous or equally-balanced competitors (a basic condition for 'perfect' competition in which no player can have
   a significant effect upon the interplay between supply and
   demand).
2. Slow industry growth: natural growth doesn't offer scope
   for the individual firm's ambition, with the consequence
   that its growth can only be achieved at the expense of its
   rivals.
3. High fixed or storage costs relative to the value added.
4. Lack of differentiation or switching costs.

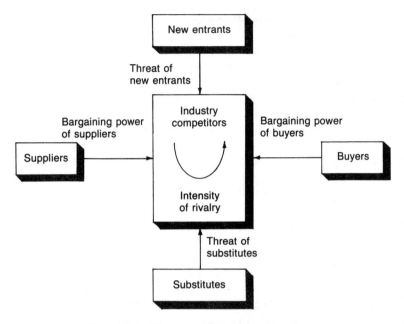

Figure 8.1 Elements of Industry Structure

5. Capacity augmented in large increments, for example steel or shipbuilding.
6. Diverse competitors — particularly international rivals.
7. High strategic stakes.
8. High exit barriers, for example specialised assets with low liquidation values, redundancy costs, social implications, etc.

To cope with these pressures, each firm will seek to develop a strategy which will enable it to succeed — usually at the expense of its competitors — and Porter distinguishes three 'general strategic approaches' which are available: overall cost leadership, differentiation and focus. (These have been designated by other authors as an undifferentiated, differentiated or concentrated marketing strategy, respectively.) While each of these strategies represents a radically different approach to the market, it has become increasingly accepted that selection and effective implementation of the most appropriate strategy depends heavily upon a marketing orientation.

In earlier chapters we have attempted to define the nature of a marketing orientation and show how it has evolved from other, rather different managerial orientations which preceded it. Few people have difficulty in accepting the fundamental proposition on which marketing is founded — 'The purpose of an enterprise is to create and keep a customer' — indeed, many consider it so self-evident as not to be worth stating. However, given the existence of rapidly expanding markets due to population growth, few managers or companies found it necessary to examine further the implications of this cardinal principle for success. Ted Levitt (1977), the godfather of modern marketing, developed this cardinal principle as demanding:

[a] few simple things about the requisites of success:

1. To do that [create and keep a customer] you have to produce and deliver goods and services that people want and value at prices and under conditions that are reasonably attractive relative to those offered by others to a proportion of customers large enough to make those prices and conditions possible.
2. To continue to do that, the enterprise must produce revenue in excess of costs in sufficient abundance and with sufficient regularity to attract, keep, and develop capital for the enterprise, and to keep at least abreast and sometimes ahead of competitive offerings.
3. No enterprise, no matter how small, can do any of this by mere instinct or accident. It has to clarify its purposes, strategies, and plans, and the larger the enterprise the greater the necessity that these be clearly written down, clearly communicated, and frequently reviewed by the senior members of the enterprise.
4. And in all cases, there must be an appropriate system of rewards, audits, and controls to assure that what's intended gets properly done, and when not, that it gets quickly rectified.

In essence, then, the marketing philosophy or orientation is encapsulated in proposition 1 above, while propositions 2, 3 and 4 spell out the requirements for effective implementation. As we have seen in Chapter 4, there is no shortage of advice as to the correlates of success or critical success factors of the following kind:

1. Reflect commitment to the philosophy of marketing in the firm's top positions.
2. Have clear, measurable statements of the company's long-term objectives.

3. Adopt a long-term approach to achieve profitability
   through satisfying market needs.
4. Focus on customer needs: research markets and make
   innovations market-relevant.
5. Add value before increasing price.
6. Pay attention to quality: quality of products and quality of
   service.
7. Take responsibility for products after they leave the factory gates.
8. Be committed to after-sales service.
9. Have strong marketing communications with the target
   market.

On inspection, however, and as our findings in Chapter 6 confirmed, few of the claimed factors actively discriminate between
the successful and less successful firms. The reason for this is to
be found in two seminal articles, whose analysis and prognosis
is as apposite today as it was in 1960 when Ted Levitt published
'Marketing Myopia' and 1970 when B. Charles Ames published
'Trappings vs Substance in Industrial Marketing'.

Levitt's 'Marketing Myopia' opens with the trenchant observation that, 'Every declining industry was once a growth industry', and proceeds to analyse what it is that results in formerly
successful industries and firms becoming failures. Essentially,
Levitt's thesis is that firms become successful by offering a product or service which is better at meeting the needs of consumers
than are other available substitute products. But, having displaced
earlier substitutes, and self-satisfied with its new found success,
the firm becomes complacent and fails to realise that its product
or service can be further improved. Failing to make this improvement itself, the firm becomes vulnerable to the innovator who
appreciates that customer needs can be better satisfied by a new
product and sets about creating that product. Thus, consumers
have a fairly limited set of basic needs such as food and shelter,
health, security, transportation, recreation, entertainment, and
so on, but each of these can be satisfied in an almost infinite
variety of ways. Given that the consumer is motivated by self-
interest and has no particular obligation or loyalty to any given
supplier, then he will transfer his patronage to whichever supplier offers him the greatest value as perceived by himself. When

exchange was direct between producer and user the former was able to develop a fairly good understanding of the latter's needs but with task specialisation and industrialisation, producer and user are rarely in direct contact, with the result that producers can but infer users' needs unless they re-establish a dialogue with them. Marketing is all about establishing that dialogue and means that supply decisions will be based upon a deliberate attempt to identify and define specific consumer needs. The marketing concept, philosophy or orientation demands that all the firms' actions start and finish with the consumer while the marketing function is the business activity responsible for initiating and sustaining the dialogue with the customer.

As a concept, or business philosophy, marketing is deceptively simple — so much so that many firms and CEOs have failed fully to grasp its implications. It was this failure which prompted Ames to pen 'Trappings vs Substance in Industrial Marketing' in response to a groundswell of criticism from industrial companies that, while marketing might work for firms selling consumer goods like soap, detergents, packaged goods and the like, it had little to offer the firm making industrial products. According to Ames, this view arose because the critics had failed to appreciate the *substance* of the marketing concept and had mistaken this for the *trappings* of marketing activity, such as advertising and promotion. Specifically, Ames cited the following as typical of the 'trappings' he had observed in industrial goods companies:

Declarations of support from top management — speeches, annual reports.

Creation of a marketing organisation — appointment of a marketing head and product or market managers, transfer to marketing of the product development and service functions, establishment of a market research function, salesmen reassigned round markets, advertising function strengthened.

Adoption of new administrative mechanisms — formal marketing planning approaches, more and better sales information, reporting system restructured around markets.

Increased marketing expenditures — staffing, training and development, advertising research.

But as Ames continued to point out: 'These moves ... by themselves are no guarantee of marketing success. The kind of

Table 8.1 Ames' 10 Questions for Identifying the Substantive
Nature of Marketing

'Can you describe at least three feasible strategic focuses that have
been evaluated and seriously considered for each of your product/
market businesses?

Can you cite specific steps your marketing department has taken
over the past three years that effectively blocked the competitive
threat of international as well as domestic competitors?

Can you cite changes in the specifications or characteristics of your
product/service package that are linked directly to the identification
of changing needs in specific customer segments?

Is there an effective interchange of ideas among your marketing,
operating and financial functions in both the development of
product/market strategy and the execution of it? Is top management
actively involved in this process?

Do you have an organized channel of communication to ensure that
the views of those men working most closely with the customers
are taken into account in identifying product needs and
opportunities?

Do you have a clear picture of the relative profit contribution from
sales of individual items to all of your customer channel/segments?

Have you, within the last 12 months, evaluated — and made a
conscious decision whether to drop or retain — those products that
account for less than 10% of sales and profits?

Have you made a comparison of your economics and those of your
competitors, as well as a comparative value analysis of all individual
items where you compete head-to-head?

Are your marketing organisation and your planning and control
systems designed around end-use market characteristics?

Can you honestly say that four out of every five men filling your
top marketing positions are serious candidates for future general
management jobs?'

Source: Ames (1970).

change that is needed is a fundamental shift in thinking and attitude throughout the company so that everyone in every functional area places paramount importance on being responsive to
market needs'. In order to help define the substance of marketing,
Ames posed the 10 questions (reproduced in Table 8.1), each of

Table 8.2 The Ten Market Commandments

1.	Acceptance by the chief executive of the organisation that customers are the ultimate determinant of its success or failure.
2.	Having a clearly defined mission and set of objectives which are understood and accepted throughout the organisation.
3.	Having a deep understanding, as opposed to simply a knowledge, of what influences the environment and markets in which the company operates.
4.	Assessing honestly the positive and negative assets of the company.
5.	Identifying the particular segments or niches where real opportunities exist for the company.
6.	Knowing the direct and indirect competition, what makes it tick, and how it is likely to act and react.
7.	Establishing the competitive edge which will make customers choose the products or services against those of the competition.
8.	Bringing an open-minded perception to interpreting, developing and presenting the product, and the facilities and organisation to support it.
9.	Marketenvolk — selection, training and motivation of performers.
10.	Total dedication to the achievement of corporate success in the market-place and of overall company objectives.

Source: McBurnie and Clutterbuck (1988).

which addresses a specific aspect of marketing practice, but underlying them all is the question of *commitment* — particularly on the part of the Chief Executive. This requirement was confirmed strongly in a recent in-depth analysis of factors associated with successful performance in a number of UK companies by McBurnie & Clutterbuck (1988) who found that: the most successful chief executives have a market-place orientation and commitment; this is an attitude of mind, not the result of a particular background or discipline; and this attitude is essential — whether the business is consumer, industrial or service. The detailed findings from the case studies led the authors to propose the 'Ten Market Commandments' set out in Table 8.2, which they then reduced to the 3 'C's of marketing: *culture, creativity* and *commitment* — to which we would add a fourth 'C', *customer*.

But, as noted above, simple though the marketing concept appears to be in principle, and significant though the rewards are claimed to be in practice, many individuals and organisations appear to experience great difficulty in adopting the concept. In a study published in 1981, McNamara identified five factors which appeared to have hampered the adoption and implementation of the concept:

    (i)   confusion about the meaning of the concept and its implications;

   (ii)   top managements lack of exposure to marketing principles;

  (iii)   inability to hire appropriate marketing managers;

  (iv)   lack of appropriate organisational structures, systems and procedures;

   (v)   resistance to change.

In the period since the publication of these findings, considerable progress has been made to clarify the concept, provide appreciation courses for top managers and increase the cadre of professional marketers through appropriate undergraduate and postgraduate marketing education and training. Similar advances have also been made in devising structures and procedures, so that one is drawn inevitably to the conclusion that any overall lack of progress must be attributed largely to the last factor — resistance to change — which brings us full circle to the point made earlier, that if we wish to change behaviour we first need to achieve an attitudinal change.

Writing in 1986, Jay Lorsch, a Harvard Business School professor with a distinguished record in diagnosing and solving corporate organisational problems, identified four stages in the accomplishment of fundamental change: *awareness, confusion, development of strategic vision* and *experimentation*. Our own research suggests that successful companies have completed this sequence while less successful companies have yet to start, or have only progressed part way. As we have seen, *awareness* is frequently dulled because companies have become complacent after past successes and so fail to recognise the warning signals when change is imminent ('Marketing Myopia'). As a result, awareness often results only as a consequence of a dramatic event or crisis in the fortunes of the company which precipitates the *confusion* stage. Numerous case studies attest to the fact that the serving management, and particularly the CEO, are frequently ill-equipped to deal with the crisis and the history of the 'survivors' suggests that the appointment of a new CEO is often the necessary catalyst to prompt the definition of a new corporate direction. This new sense of direction is almost always the consequence of Lorsch's third stage — the *development of strategic vision* — and is frequently published in a formal way in a corporate vision or mission statement. Warren Bennis (1969) provides perhaps the best explanation of precisely what this is or should be:

> What is a vision? A vision should state what the future of the organisation will be like. It should engage our hearts and our spirits, it is an assertion about what we and our colleagues want to create. It is something worth going for; it provides meaning to the people in the organisation, in the work they are doing. By its definition, a vision is a little cloudy and grand; if it were clear it wouldn't be a vision. It is a living document that can always be added to; it is a starting place to get more and more levels of specificity. Now beyond that, when the vision statement is close to completion, the questions that also have to be asked in any organisation are: 'What is unique about us? What values are true priorities for the next era? What would make me personally commit my mind and heart to this vision over the next ten years? What does the world really need that our organisation can and should provide? and What do I really want my organisation to accomplish so that I will be committed, aligned and proud of my association with the institution?'

Once such a mission statement has been articulated, the organisation can move on to Lorsch's fourth stage of *experimentation* through the gradual commitment of people and money to the new sense of direction.

Now, the difficulty in achieving this is that such changes of direction usually involve a change in the corporate culture which has been defined by Uttal (1983) as: 'A system of shared values (what is important) and beliefs (how things work) that interact with a company's people, or organisational structures and control systems to produce behavioural norms (the way we do things around here)'. In a similar vein, Schein (1985) defines corporate culture as:

> The pattern of basic assumptions that a given group has invented, discovered or developed in learning to cope with its problems of external adaptation and internal integration — a pattern of assumptions that has worked well enough to be considered valid and, therefore, to be taught to new members as the correct way to perceive, think and feel in relation to these problems.

Clearly, if one is forced to propose a radical change in the corporate culture to meet new competitive challenges then one is likely to encounter strong resistance to change. Indeed, it is only when faced with crises of the kind provided by the oil price increases of the 1970s, and the recessions they provoked, that many organisations become willing to consider radical change as necessary for survival, let alone success. Thus, while the benefits of a customer orientation and being market driven have long been apparent to consistently successful companies such as Unilever, Philips, Du Pont, 3M, Marks & Spencer, etc., it required the competitive pressures of the seventies and eighties to persuade most companies to switch from a production, sales or financial orientation to a marketing orientation.

The dramatic effect of these external pressures is nowhere more apparent than in the profound changes that have swept through Britain's industrial base over the last decade. In the main, UK companies have been forced to rationalise their operations. It is now time for these companies to strive to consolidate and advance

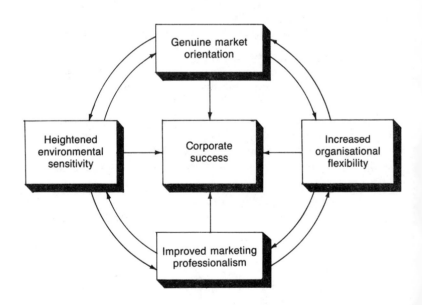

Figure 8.2 Virtuous Circle of Best Marketing Practice

with an approach to business based on adding value that is meaningful to customers, thus increasing their perceived utility of the goods they buy. To maximise these efforts, it is necessary to develop skills that allow them to fuse technical ability with market need in order to create unique and superior products that will, in turn, result in a sustainable competitive advantage.

Given this change in the economic and competitive climate in the UK (and elsewhere) it is confidently expected that more and more companies will adopt the marketing concept and seek to achieve Hooley *et al*'s, 'virtuous circle of best marketing practice' (Figure 8.2). Finally, while we cannot claim that marketing and a marketing orientation will guarantee competitive success, we are convinced that their absence will result in failure.

References

Ames, B.C. (1970) 'Trappings versus substance in industrial marketing', *Harvard Business Review*, July/August.
Bennis, Warren (1969) *Organization Development*, Addison-Wesley.
Levitt, T. (1960) 'Marketing myopia', *Harvard Business Review*.
Levitt, T. (1977) 'Marketing and the corporate purpose' in J. Backman and J. Czepeil (eds) (1977) *Changing Marketing Strategies in a New Economy*, Ross-Merrill Education Publishing.
Lorsch, J.W. (1986) 'Managing culture: the invisible barrier to strategic change', *California Management Review*, vol. 28, no. 2.
McBurnie, A. and Clutterbuck, D. (1988) *The Marketing Edge*, Penguin Business Books.
Porter, M. (1979) 'How competitive forces shape strategy', *Harvard Business Review*, March/April.
Porter, M. (1980) *Competitive Strategy*, The Free Press.
Schein, E.H. (1985) *Organizational Culture: A Dynamic View*, Jossey-Bass, San Francisco.
Scott, B. (1984) 'National strategy for stronger US competitiveness', *Harvard Business Review*, March/April.
Uttal, B. (1983) 'The corporate culture vulture', *Fortune*, 17 October.

Index

While all the subject references are included in this index, the author references to Chapter 4 have been excluded as there are more than 160 entries. These will be found on pp. 101–8.

MOUNT PLEASANT LIBRARY
TEL. 051 207 3581 Ext. 3701